BUT I DIGRESS

a collection of short stories and tall tales

PETER BRIDGFORD

I HOPE THESE SILLY STORIES
PUT A GRIN ON YOUR FACE!

BUT I DIGRESS —

BRIDGE

But I Digress

ISBN: 978-1-940244-96-9

Illustration: "Pandora's Box" by Betz
www.etamcru.com/bezt/pandora-box-1#
www.facebook.com/etam.grupa
bezt.etam@gmail.com

Cover Design
Amy Files

Designed and Produced by
Indie Author Warehouse
12 High Street, Thomaston, Maine 04861
www.indieauthorwarehouse.com
Printed in the United States of America

This book is dedicated to Celeste Bridgford. If it were not for her gentle insistence to get these stories written down and to try a new genre, this collection would never have taken form. It would have existed only in the ether of my faded memories like the cinematic classic *Sasquatch: The Legend of Bigfoot*, the classy Buffalo Bill, Lou Piccone #89, and the greatest rock band of all time—Rush.

Contents

Introduction

The tales in this collections are the stories that I spun during my lunch duties over the course of an elementary and middle school teaching career that spanned nearly twenty years. It was during these brief twenty- to thirty-minute sessions in front of a rapt young audience demanding entertainment that I was forced to develop some kind of storytelling skills. I began retelling memories of my youth, even though many of them were partially forgotten or even repressed. I found out that, in spite of my concern that they were going to be too plain to be captivating, there was something universal in these stories that appealed to my young listeners. In fact, if I ran out of time before I finished a story, which happened quite often, the children insisted that I pick it up the next time at the very point where I'd left off. Eventually, the stories gained enough notoriety to be known by their straightforward monikers, like the Halloween Story, the Farting Horse Story, the Poop Your Pants Story, or the Want to Know What We Do to Boys Like You in Prison? Story.

These are all based on true events of my teenage years and my twenties. What I discovered from telling them over the years is that they change as rapidly as sandbars in a fast-moving river. For example, if I was with group of students who were enthused by gore, I knew that I should emphasize the yuck factor more. However, if I were with an older group of tweens and teens, I brought out the rebellious and risk facts more. It's important to note that these stories were never told sitting down. I was always pacing in front of the room, adding illustrations for effect, and using wild accents and gestures to engage the audience as much as I could. So, as you read these somewhat sterile printed versions, feel free to stand up and start walking around while you read them with as much animation as you can muster. Now, this might be weird if you're in the library or taking public transportation, but that's okay—the liveliness of these stories needs to be retained at all costs.

Also note that the language in these stories is pretty tame. Since I was telling them to an audience ranging from seven to fifteen years old, I tried to use words that didn't get too racy, even if the subject matter did. That being said, I flirted with disaster by telling some pretty salty tales that may or may not have been questionable in their age-appropriateness. However, I was repeatedly informed by parents that the retelling of my stories had become a major part of their dinner table conversations and family discussions. Universally, there seemed to be nothing but amusement over having their children passionately tell stories about life on commercial fishing boats and the glory days of high school in Buffalo, New York, in the 1980s. Actually, the most pressing issue that resulted from the storytelling was the fact that the students became too enthralled to eat their lunches, and I was instructed to keep reminding them to take a bite or two every so often.

Lastly, I've been told there is no common thread among the stories in this collection—no unifying connection or theme that binds them all together. I guess that's true, but I see them as a meandering pathway of time travel from the THEN to the HERE of my life. The circuitous *Family Circus* like route of this reminds me of the drunken stumbling of the homeless guy I met in Providence, Rhode Island, but they also point to the purely Zen moment from Sesame Street when Grover succinctly informed us all that we cannot be HERE and THERE at the same time. Truer words have never been spoken. And, as I am currently HERE, I have to look back at the THERE to figure out how in the world I made it in one piece! With those discerning lenses on, I think that the thread to these stories can be seen in the important life lessons that have lasted a lifetime.

Enjoy!

Bridge

The Last Halloween

● ● ● ● ●

When I turned fifteen, I came to one of life's unexpected and unforeseen roadblocks. Just as I began to plan my costume for Halloween, people began to hint in a heavy-handed way that I'd become too old to go trick-or-treating. At first I disregarded these naysayers, but the intensity and the frequency of their comments, and the fact that they seemed to know something I didn't, started to have a negative impact on me. If there was an unspoken rule about the age limit for participating in the activities of this holiday, I hadn't heard anything about it. But apparently, it was the rule, and, being a rule-following good boy, I reluctantly accepted this decree.

But as the holiday approached, my friends Paolo and Viola, who'd had the same shock over the whole issue, came to me to talk about the matter. As we bemoaned the fact that we were no longer allowed to be included in a ritual that we held close to our hearts, we all came to the conclusion that the three main purposes of Halloween—getting dressed up, getting candy, and having fun—were, in fact, completely and utterly free from age restrictions. There was no real reason that we couldn't go trick-or-treating as teenagers, and so we decided to participate in Halloween again. Even though we knew that we were going to endure a relentless barrage of insults and put-downs from our peers and the adults in our lives to badger and bully us into compliance with a societal norm, we didn't care—we were going to go trick-or-treating!

Because we'd made our decision so late, we all had to throw our costumes together. For me, this was no problem. I took my grandfather's long tweed raincoat, a rubber clown mask, and the battered fedora that I wore, and *voilà!*—an instant costume. I didn't know what I was, exactly, but I didn't feel any need to justify or identify my costume to anyone as I grabbed a large plastic shopping bag and proudly walked out of my house looking like some kind of creepy clown. Our plan was to meet up at Viola's house because it was an equidistant walk for both Paolo and me and because it was surrounded by big old houses that were perfect for a very lucrative trick-or-treating takeaway.

Back in those days, the neighborhoods of Buffalo, New York, had a unique solution to dealing with the autumn leaves. Residents were encouraged to rake their yards into a collective pile of leaves at curbside for a giant vacuum truck to suck up later. As a result, there were massive piles of leaves lining the streets, easily standing waist high and six feet wide. Such landmarks were too perfect a target to ignore.

So, as soon as our trio had come together and we encountered our first magnificent leaf pile, I decided I needed to do an epic jump into it. I took off running as fast as I could, and as I got near my target, I ceased being a silly teenager and became an Olympic long-jumper. I committed wholly and launched myself, feet first, right into the pile. It was so huge, I completely disappeared inside it with an eruption of leaves. When I reemerged, I was laughing uncontrollably. This whole process—the frantic running up to the pile, the fearless leaping into it, and the resulting leaf explosion—was so exhilarating and so exemplified the fact that this last experience of our youth was on borrowed time, I swore I would jump into each and every leaf pile I saw throughout the night. And I set out to make sure that I made this declaration come true.

The actual act of trick-or-treating that night, however, turned out to be more difficult than we had anticipated. After we'd rung the doorbell, yelled out our greeting, and held out our bags with the usual excitement, we bubbled with hope for the anticipated candy gift. But as soon as the door opened up and the homeowners saw three tall and gawky teenagers standing there, they all had the same exact response: their initial inviting grins, prepared for the sight of little kids in cute costumes, faded as their eyes took in our nearly full-grown statures. Then their eyes invariably scanned for the necessary child they were sure was hiding behind us. But when they didn't see anyone else there, their faces soured into angry scowls and they pulled back their bowls of confectionary offerings as they hissed, "Aren't you too old to be trick-or-treating?"

In a calm and rational way, we came up with an appropriate response to this charge. We explained that, since Halloween was about dressing up, having fun, and getting candy, it was, in fact, an ageless activity. And just because we had crossed some arbitrary chronological boundary didn't mean that we didn't like to do those things anymore. We ended our thoughtful discourse by saying that the whole holiday had less to do with the dates on our birth certificates and more to do with how young we felt in our hearts!

I don't know if it was our calmness in the face of their criticism or the underlying truth of our argument, but each homeowner slowly relented and allowed us to take the candy, albeit with body language that said this would be the last time they'd ever give us any. This same routine happened each and every time we came to a house, so we became very adept at defending ourselves with our speech, and, in the end, we weren't turned away or denied candy from a single home all night.

After many leaf pile jumps and a successful procurement of Halloween bounty, we came to THE house. Every neighborhood has one—the old house with the dreary, disheveled exterior and the creepy owners that has gained irrefutable status as the haunted house avoided by small children. We had come to that house now. The old three-story brick structure sat strong and menacing in front of us, and its heavy slate roofs appeared to be pushing it down and keeping it in place. The building's dirty exterior absorbed the night's darkness and created sinister shadows that took on the shapes of terrifying gargoyles. In fact, the house looked so scary that we were all prepared to skip it and head to the next one. But then we saw that the porch light was on.

The universally accepted and time-honored tradition states that, on Halloween, if the porch light is on, the homeowners want trick-or-treaters. The converse is also true: if the porch light is off, stay away. All kids know the reason for this: if the porch light is off, it's a clear indication that the inhabitants are not home, are fundamentalist Christians who believe that celebrating a pagan holiday is a sin, or don't have any candy, or just wish to be left the hell alone. Most sane kids know this and follow the rule—and we certainly did!

So, even though this house was like a scary set from a horror movie, because the porch light was on, we had ourselves an instant conundrum: should we skip and go to a safer house, or should we knock on the door to get some more candy? We huddled to decide what we were going to do. Despite the real possibility of encountering cannibals, devil worshipers, Bible-thumpers, or evil spirits, we finally came to the conclusion that the porch light was beckoning us like moths. When we got to the front steps and started up them, they creaked hauntingly. We huddled again—just for a quick recount of our votes. And like competing auctioneers, we all whispered our sentiments.

"Do you think we should do this?"

"I dunno."

"The porch light *is* on."

"Yeah, but the house is really *scary!*"

"So should we do this?"

"Yeah."

"I dunno."

"Should we?"

"I guess. I dunno."

"Okay, let's go."

When the porch groaned pitifully under our steps, we called for another huddle and another whispered debate.

"Do you really think we should do this?"

"I dunno."

"The porch light *is* on."

"Yeah, but this house is *really* scary!"

"So should we do this?"

"Yeah."

"I dunno."

"Should we?"

"I guess. I dunno."

"Okay, let's go."

We made our way across the porch to the front door. There was no doorbell, just a huge iron knocker. We used it to bang loudly on the door, and when no one answered immediately, we got ready to make a hasty retreat off the groaning porch, down the creaking steps, and far,

far away from this haunted place. But a light went on inside and the door slowly opened, revealing a man who bore an eerie resemblance to Mr. Burns in *The Simpsons*. He was so old and gaunt, the skin of his bald skull stretched as taut as a drumhead. There were liver spots on his claw-like hands. And he answered the door with a scowl that quickly twisted into a sneer as his raspy old-man voice squeaked, "Aren't you too old to be trick-or-treating?"

We gave him our spiel, but our voices were tight with fear as we said it. The man looked us up and down, then turned around and brought forth a bowl from the shadows. He reached in with his skeletal talon and grabbed something to give to us. We thrust our bags forward to receive his gift, and, once we had it and said a quick thank-you, we turned to flee before he ate our livers. The porch groaned and the steps creaked, and we ambled quickly away to stand under the safety of the nearest streetlight to calm ourselves down after our brush with death.

It was only then that we looked to see what the ghoulish old man had given us. Not only is it considered rude to check the treat given at the door, but in this case, we wanted to be well clear of the evil dwelling with the creepy old man before we did so. We grabbed the last item in our bags and pulled it out to look at it in the light. He had given each of us a small white rubber mouse.

Let's review something here. What's the real purpose of Halloween? Sure, dressing up and having fun are both important, but the *real* reason is to get **candy.** Lots and lots of candy. In all the years of trick-or-treating, I had received a cornucopia of homemade and commercially available chocolate bars, taffy, candy corn, lollipops, baked goods, popcorn balls, peanuts, and even apples—which, of course, due to the urban legend of insane weirdos putting razor blades into them, we always tossed right into the bushes. But the point of Halloween is to get as much candy as you can carry. So who in their right mind gives out white rubber mice? Nobody. Nobody in their right mind would ever think that kids would want a stupid rubber mouse on Halloween! It's insane, and it borders on the cruel and unusual to hand an expectant child on Halloween night a rubber mouse when all they want is **candy.**

Paolo and Viola seemed to shrug off this atrocity and continued on to the next street of houses, but I just couldn't let it go. In fact, I'd begun to work myself up into a froth over the inanity *(or insanity)* of handing out rubber mice on Halloween. And it was at this moment that one of the top five stupidest ideas came into my head. I know it deserves this moniker because this thought has never even *pretended* to form itself, before or since. For some inexplicable reason, I made the incredibly stupid decision to throw the rubber mouse at the next car that drove by! I truly have no idea where this idea came from, and to this very day, I chalk it up to some kind of contagion passed to me by the evil old man. There can be no other rational way to explain such an idiotic thought.

So, when I heard the sounds of an approaching vehicle behind me, I did not look back, but instead did my best imitation of Fernando Valenzuela. While Paolo and Viola continued walking ahead of me, completely unaware of my ridiculous plan, I struck the pose of a pitcher on the mound. I had never played a real baseball game in my life, but, as I heard the approaching vehicle getting closer and closer, I slowly drew my leg up for a perfect pitching windup, cocked my right arm with the mouse comfortably in my grip, and got ready to make my throw. When my ears registered that the car was abreast of me, I spun 270 degrees and hurled the mouse with an amazing follow-through.

As a kid, I was blessed with a strong arm. I never played football or baseball on any organized team, but my ability to throw with great velocity had made me one of the first picks in any playground game or in phys ed class at school. Unfortunately, *aiming* my throws was not my strongest suit. I could throw a ball hard and far, but I usually couldn't hit the side of a barn. If you needed someone to throw a Hail Mary pass in a football game or throw rapidly in a dodgeball game, I was your man. But if you needed someone who could actually hit a specific target, well, that wasn't me.

But as the rubber mouse left my hand that night, I had two instant realizations: I was going to hit my target this time, and it was not a car, but a panel van. The mouse flew with the accuracy of a laser-guided missile and struck the vehicle squarely on the side. And like a giant rolling steel drum, the side of the van made a deafening clang as the rubber mouse found its mark. The next sound that shattered the night was the van screeching to a stop. The door flew open, the driver jumped out, and his screaming curses spewed forth into the night's darkness.

The fact that I had been stupid enough to throw the rubber mouse at all was only eclipsed by the shock that I'd actually hit my target. My synapses were so overwhelmed in their attempt to process what had just happened that time slowed to the point where I could hear the blinking of my eyelids. So when I turned to yell to Paolo and Viola that we should run away *now*, all I saw was their backsides far ahead of me, fleeing for their lives. As the van driver began to threaten to kill me, my friends, my family, and everyone I'd ever met in my life, I recovered enough to know that I needed to get the hell out of there!

All of this had taken place just outside a prestigious girls' school. There was a driveway that led toward the school buildings to my left, and since that was where I had last seen my friends headed, I set off running in that direction. The adrenaline of the moment made me run like I never had before. I lifted my knees high like a Lipizzaner stallion while I held onto my hat with one hand. And I was running with such pure panic, I didn't realize that the driveway was actually a horseshoe-shaped road that parents used to drop off and pick up their daughters from the school. So there I was, one hand holding down my fedora, the other clutching my bag of candy, and my long raincoat flopping wildly with my exaggerated strides as I ran blindly straight back toward the very van driver who was still shouting curses and issuing threats beside his stopped vehicle. As a matter of fact, if Paolo and Viola hadn't called out from their hiding place in the shrubbery, I would have run right around and smacked into the man.

The three of us hid there, panting from fear and exertion, while we listened to the driver spend all of his rage. He wasn't about to chase after anyone, so when he'd cursed enough, he got back in his van and drove off. I breathed a sigh of relief after surviving such a life-threatening experience, and when I looked over at my friends, their eyes were locked onto me. In unison, they shouted, "That was the stupidest thing you've ever done!"

The rest of the night was uneventful and just pure fun. The trick-or-treating continued to require our explanation as to why we weren't too old, and the gigantic leaf piles were still too inviting to pass up. When we'd had our fill, we headed back to our starting point, said good night, and set off to our own homes.

My parents were in the living room watching television. I knew they would want to try to intercept me to enforce some kind of rationing of my candy intake, and I was determined not to let that happen. So I quietly opened and shut the front door and got to the stairs before I yelled out to them that I was home and was going straight to bed. I walked triumphantly into my messy room, shut the door, and got ready to enjoy the fruits of my labor. If the real purpose of Halloween is to get candy, then I was going to savor that until I was close to vomiting. It is, after all, mandatory in the true tradition of Halloween to not only sate the sugar craving, but to do so to excess!

I sat down on my bed and reached into my bag. I had high hopes of finding a $100,000 bar, my favorite type of chocolate bar. I mean, if I pulled out a Hershey bar, a Snickers, a Three Musketeers, a Mars Bar, or a Reese's Peanut Butter Cup, that'd be fine, too. But I really hoped there would be a $100,000 bar! My hand descended into the cache, my fingertips primed to ascertain the type of candy from the shape and feel of its wrapper. But I didn't touch any candy. Instead, my hand grabbed a bunch of leaves. I took these and threw them right into my trash can. I was not going to let anything ruin the enjoyment of my sweet, sweet rewards, so with great anticipation I reached back into the bag—maybe it would Smartees or M&M's or red licorice this time. But my hand touched nothing but leaves again. I pulled out another clump and put them in the trash can. Foolishly holding onto the fantasy that the third time was the charm, I put my hand back into the bag in hopes of touching any kind of candy, even if it was black licorice, but all I could feel were leaves.

I opened the bag wider and nearly stuck my entire head inside. There was nothing in there but leaves. I could not believe my eyes. I started to scoop out the leaves to find the candy, but when the trash can was full and my bag was empty, I understood with painful clarity what had happened. Each time I'd jumped into one of those massive leaf piles, my candy bag had opened up enough for the candy to fall out and the leaves to fall in. And since I hadn't checked my bag throughout the night (except to discover that stupid mouse), it always felt full. I had no choice now but to sigh deeply, turn off the light, and go to bed without so much as one piece of candy.

And that was the last time I ever went trick-or-treating.

But I digress...

Calling Alligators

• • • • •

I attended the Calasanctius School for most of my elementary, middle, and high school years. This wacky institution was not only a pioneer in gifted education, but it also had a field trip program that was decades ahead of its time. Nowadays, there's a plethora of educational institutions that have travel and expeditions as part of their curriculum, but back in those days, Calasanctius was wholly unique. Every school year, we students were herded onboard an old junker of a school bus to travel to the distant corners of the United States, Canada, or Mexico. The impact of these field trips was huge on my development as a young man, and they created profound and ingrained memories that still continue to influence me. And although there were some moments on Cal's field trips when the students were at risk, the independence and interpersonal skills that were honed by the forced cohabitation, exploration, and problem solving has served me well throughout the years as a teacher and a parent.

This particular trip lasted nearly three weeks and involved a journey down the East Coast. Along the way, we visited the cities of Philadelphia, Washington, and Savannah before heading down the entire length of the Sunshine State. During our stop in St. Augustine, Florida, we toured the historical Castillo de San Marcos before heading over to Ross Allen's Alligator Farm. The ancient fort was really interesting and informative, but my friends and I were most excited to see the much cooler reptiles at the alligator farm. And as soon as we got there, we headed straight for the glassed-in enclosure to watch the snake handlers milk various cobras, kraits, and rattlesnakes for the making of antivenins. After this, we stood dangerously close to a gigantic saltwater crocodile just so we could take pictures with our Kodak Instamatics.

An announcement was made over the park's loudspeakers that the next lecture about alligators was going to take place in ten minutes, so we hustled over to the amphitheater to get good seats. During this interesting presentation, we learned some incredible facts about these misunderstood creatures—like they can run faster than a horse over short distances, the temperature of their nests determines the gender of the hatchlings inside their eggs, and they communicate through a series of grunts and other noises. The presenter then taught the audience how to call an alligator. According to him, by saying "Ow, ow, ow" down deep in your throat and moving your open mouth, you can actually duplicate their callings and get gators to come closer. As the crowd practiced this together, I'm sure we all looked and sounded absolutely ridiculous.

My friends and I continued to explore the park until we came to the main alligator exhibit. It consisted of a giant pond that was full of gators. Although the large enclosure was impressive, most of the alligators were lying like blackened logs on the banks of a small island in the middle and on the shoreline of the pond. A low wooden boardwalk crossed the pond, and we went out to the middle of this to get a closer look at an alligator. But they all remained too far away and seemingly lifeless as they sunned. We were frustrated by this, so we decided to use the call we'd learned in the lecture to get them to come closer.

Nothing happened. We continued to chant "Ow, ow, ow," but we began to wonder if the whole thing had just been a way to make fools out of us. But then we noticed that some of the alligators on the shore were silently slipping into the water to join the ones that were already swimming directly toward us! We knew we were safe there on the boardwalk, but the sight of that many alligators approaching us made our guts clench. We held our ground until we were surrounded, and then we started shooting close-ups. When we were finally unnerved by the proximity of the creatures below us, we skittered down the boardwalk and back to terra firma.

Our field trip continued southward and included a visit to the Magic Kingdom and EPCOT at Disney World before reaching our final destination—Everglades National Park. After the boisterous experience of a day at Disney, the sparseness and openness of the "River of Grass" was beyond our understanding. As a matter of fact, as we set up our tents in a campground in the midst of a flat and endless scrub plateau, many of us openly expressed our feelings of discontent and boredom.

That's when the leader of the trip, Ned, encouraged a few of us to go off exploring to find something that would break up the monotony of the terrain and provide a little amusement. Joe, a big Irish kid I was friends with, found a baby snake near a log. It was very tiny—about half the size of a length of fettuccine! As he held it tenderly in his big freckled hands, my friend Bobby, who had wanted to be a herpetologist when he grew up, said, "Uh, Joe, I'd be careful with that one."

Joe replied sarcastically, "What's it going to do to me, Bobby, gum me to death?"

The words were barely out of his mouth when the tiny snake bit him. Although the baby's teeth weren't very big, they were sharp enough to draw blood. Joe's instinctive reaction was to scream and shake his hand violently in an attempt to shed the baby snake. Of course, this only drove the teeth in deeper. Finally, Bobby had to come over and calm Joe down so he could slowly and gently disengage the snake from his thumb. Once this was accomplished, the snake seemed fine, Joe seemed fine, and we had all had a good laugh. Some of our boredom had been temporarily assuaged.

But when Ned saw that our lethargy was returning, he offered to lead a group of us on a walk down a dirt road that exited the campground and ventured straight into the brush. Seeing a chance for some real adventure, the boys excitedly agreed to join him, and we set off like a bunch of puppies bounding at his heels. We came upon a small pond and lined up along the shoreline to take a good look at it. To our surprise, the surface of the pond seemed to be churning with countless small animals. They were less than a foot in length, and it took us a while to figure out what they were…baby alligators.

Once we had identified them, we were barely able to contain our excitement. Someone suggested that we start calling them like we'd been taught at the alligator farm, so we all broke into a rousing chorus of "Ow, ow, ow" at the top of our lungs. Just as before, it took a moment or two before these baby alligators began to respond, but ultimately they did. A few began swimming toward our group. Then more and more joined in, until they became an ominous flotilla coming straight at us. Baby alligators can be cute, but there is something coldly sinister about them, too. When our enthusiasm started to fade at the daunting sight and our chorus weakened a little, Ned hoarsely whispered, "Come on, keep calling them, keep calling them."

As the baby alligators got within ten feet of the shore upon which we stood, each and every boy in the group had the same exact thought: if there are that many babies in this pond, where is their mother? And, as if she could read our minds, Big Mama surfaced like a breaching submarine just behind the babies and started swimming toward us!

Her sudden appearance completely silenced us, but Ned urged us to start again. "Keep calling. Keep calling."

So we did. The first wave of babies was now only five feet away, but Mama was using her strong tail to make up lost ground, and she was now within ten feet of us. With the knowledge that alligators can run for short distances faster than a horse, we turned to ask what Ned what we should do next. But he was gone. I briefly saw his rear end as he sprinted around the corner and back onto the dirt road. There was a pure and silent moment that came with the comprehension that we'd just been abandoned, and then someone screamed, "RUN!"

I panicked. When I spun around and started running for my life, I was so sure that the killer mama gator was right behind me, I didn't even glance back once. I stared straight ahead and ran as fast as I could away from that pond. I was in such a state of terror that I would have knocked down any of my friends and run right over them if they had gotten in my way. Truthfully, was just a matter of luck that no one got trampled or thrown to their death in that moment of mass hysteria.

Our whole group sprinted the entire way back to the campground. The fastest boys made it back quickly, but the slower kids took forever. When we were sure that no one had been eaten, we all stood there, bent over and gasping as we tried to catch our breath. Ned, with his customary smoking pipe in his mouth, was calmly sitting at the picnic table, and he let out a loud belly laugh that went on for several minutes.

To this day, I'm not sure if he was laughing at us because it wasn't as dangerous as it seemed and we were making a big deal about nothing, or because the situation was just as dangerous as it seemed and he was crazy enough to think it was funny. Either way, we all started yelling at Ned, who continued to chuckle and smoke his pipe. Eventually, we boys found some humor in the experience, too, but we spent the remainder of *that* afternoon looking down the trail, just in case Big Mama had decided to follow us back to the campsite and seek revenge for our disturbing her babies. We were not, however, bored anymore.

But I digress...

The Swim

● ● ● ● ●

While on another Calasanctius field trip, we stopped for the night at a campground in Ohio. It was in a lovely wooded, hilly area, and as our old bus bounced its way down the camp road past a scenic waterfall and a small pond, we all oohed and aahed about how the verdant hills loomed around us. Our usual routine was to arrive at a campground late in the afternoon, set up the tents, then start prepping food, cooking, and getting ready to clean up from dinner. But because we had arrived at this campground early, we had enough time after we set up our tents to have a few hours of free time. It was a beautiful warm day, and the various smaller groups within the large class began to make plans even before the bus came to a complete stop.

A few of my classmates thought they'd seen some structures up on a hillside, and they were convinced that this was a secret base of some kind. They enthusiastically set about enlisting as many of their comrades as they could for a hike to check it out. Even my close friends were being swayed by the excitement of discovering what those mysterious buildings were. But I was determined to enjoy the pond we had passed on our drive into the campground. The bus ride had been very hot and uncomfortable, so going for a swim seemed perfect. The campground took on the atmosphere of a cruise ship preparing to disperse passengers for various excursions, but with the leaders of the different trips lobbying for the distinction of having the greatest adventure...ever.

After much effort on my part, five of my friends decided to forsake the trip up the hill and go with me to the pond, but, as they walked with me in that direction, they looked over their shoulders forlornly as the other group headed up into the woods and disappeared from view.

The first thing we noticed when we walked up to the pond was that there was no real beach anywhere—only large, rough boulders ringed the water. Undaunted, we put our towels on the rocks and waded into the water. The bottom was sandy and pebbly, but the water was tepid and comfortable. A strange floating weed resembled tea leaves, and there was so much of it that when we stood up, bits clung to our skin like sprinkles on a cupcake, but this didn't bother us. We started splashing and dunking each other, and even sucked up big mouthfuls of water to spit like fountain spigots at one another. We were having a great time, and the peals of laughter and shrieks of fun filled the air.

We swam over to the waterfall and started to climb up its face. It was not completely vertical, but slanted at a very steep angle. It appeared to be manmade, and we let the rushing water cascade over us as we sat in it and talked about those serious matters that young teenagers talk about. The "seaweed" bits were also present in the rushing waters, and, after sitting in them for a while, we were forced to submerge ourselves to wash them off. It was around this time that we got a slight whiff of sulfur. It wasn't unpleasant, but there was clearly an aroma of eggs in the air. I suggested that the water must be coming from an underground spring to have that smell.

We had a thoroughly fantastic time, and headed back to our campsite. We got there at the very same time the hikers came down from their hillside excursion. We shared stories of our amazing afternoon in the pond, but the hikers' tale soon took over the spotlight. They had, indeed, made their way up the hill and found the abandoned buildings. Not only were these concrete structures sticking out from the earth, their doors led to underground hallways and entire subterranean rooms with derelict tables and chairs. Scattered around these rooms were reams of discarded documents, many of which seemed to be top secret or classified. The explorers told us how they had used flashlights to find their way through the labyrinth of rooms and walkways, and each story of discovery was topped by another one of even greater incredibleness.

Just when it seemed that the tales could not get any more fantastic, the campground's ranger stopped by for a visit, and he corroborated their claims—the group had, in fact, been exploring an abandoned military base that was well known among the locals. Although the base had not been vacated because of a crisis, the ranger made it dramatically clear that the group who had gone there had seen a once-in-a-lifetime sight.

I began to notice that the friends who had gone swimming with me were now giving me disgruntled looks, as if I'd personally kept them from a life-changing experience. I knew I had to try my best to salvage my pride, so I gleefully declared, "Yeah, well, we had an amazing time swimming in the pond!"

Those kids who'd gone up to the military base bestowed patronizing looks on me to convey their complete lack of being impressed, but the ranger frowned. He asked, "What pond?"

I found the question a bit unsettling, since the one and only pond seemed so prominent, and I was still trying to make a positive impression on the rest of my class. I grinned broadly and said, "The pond with the waterfall that we passed on the camp road. My friends and I spent the afternoon having a blast in that today!"

"Do you mean the waste-water collection facility?"

"The what?"

At this point, Ned, our trip leader, leaned toward me and said, "I think he's saying that you all went swimming in the campground's sewer today!"

My friends looked at me aghast. Thinking out loud, I sputtered, "But we were swimming in it all afternoon! And we splashed and dunked each other in it! And we spit *mouthfuls* of it at one another! And we…"

There was a mad dash to the bathrooms as all of us swimmers ran to shower off the sewage and brush our teeth. Even though we eventually felt clean again and never had any negative effects from our swim in the sewer, I'm not sure my friends ever forgave me for this escapade. What I do know is that they never again listened to any idea I had for ways to spend a free afternoon on a field trip.

But I digress…

Glory

● ● ● ● ●

As a sophomore in high school, I went on one of the more ambitious Calasanctius field trips. After driving all the way to Arizona in our ancient and iconic bus, we undertook a successful hike of the Bright Angel Trail in Grand Canyon National Park. With this accomplishment under our belts, we began the long drive back to Buffalo. Along the way, we stopped for a night at a state park campground in Colorado. As our bus lumbered its way over a culvert at the park entrance and onto the circular camp road, we took notice of the landscape and the apparent lack of other campers, and came to the conclusion that this would be the perfect location for a gigantic game of Capture the Flag. With an almost unlimited playing area and everyone involved, the proposed game became something epic and memorable while we were still bumping along to our campsite.

We set up our tents and did our chores in record time. Afterwards, we gathered together to pick teams. There was excitement in the air because we all knew that this would be no ordinary game of Capture the Flag—it would, in fact, be an event that would be spoken about for generations. And without having to say so, we all knew that the individual who helped win the game would undoubtedly become a legend in school lore!

My team's flag was positioned on the side closest to our tent sites, while the other team's flag was on the far side of the empty campground. The boundary between the two territories ran right through the grove of dense woods in the middle. As my team assigned roles and planned our strategy, the consensus was that a frontal assault was going to be the best bet. So, once the game was started, the forest in the center of the circular camp road became the main field of play. The immediate shrieks and announcements of capture made it clear that the other team had the identical strategy in mind.

But I had taken note of the layout of the campground and had designed what I considered to be a far superior plan of action. It seemed to me that if someone could flank the other team and maneuver undetected behind enemy lines, their flag would be totally unprotected—and I was just the man for the job! My idea was simple: head back toward the road, sneak down it and past the culvert, and then spring up on the other side and ambush the opponent's base from the rear! It seemed foolproof, and I was completely confident of success.

As I made my way from tree to tree like a super-spy, visions of impending victory danced in my head. If I singlehandedly won this legendary Capture the Flag game, I would ascend to a special pantheon of greatness! Although a ticker-tape parade was probably out of the question, the image of myself being boosted up on the shoulders of my celebrating teammates looped inside my brain until I was drunk on my own imagined greatness. I was willing to do whatever was necessary to become the hero I so clearly saw in those fantastical images inside my head.

As the shrieks and screams of the game continued behind me, I made my way undetected through the forest and around the camp road. When the trees thinned out and the land became grassy, I thought nothing about dropping to the ground and belly-crawling toward the ditch that ran along the road. When I got close enough, I abandoned caution, stood up, and jumped into the ditch. The three inches of foul water in the bottom of the ditch surprised me, but that didn't matter. I dropped to my belly again and crawled through the slop like an Army Ranger.

It was slow going, and by the time I neared the culvert, I was covered from head to toe in mud. But I had not been seen by anyone, which meant that everything was going according to plan. Just as I crawled up to the metal culvert pipe, I was stunned to see one of my teammates crouched there with clothes and skin similarly coated in mud. It turned out he'd had the same exact plan! I was a little disappointed that someone else had had the same brilliant idea of flanking the enemy, I was glad to have the companionship. After all, there's safety in numbers.

We began crawling through the rusty corrugated culvert. How we didn't slice ourselves and win an ambulance ride to the emergency room is beyond me, but we made our way through the slop in that metal tunnel without issue. After clearing this challenge, we continued to belly-crawl in the ditch until we came to the place that we were confident was the perfect location for our ambush. But once there, a massively important detail had to be ironed out before we could proceed. With a two-person attack, we now had the luxury of using one of us as a decoy. But which one of us would volunteer for that role? After all, the decoy was going to get caught; the non-decoy was going to get the glory. One person would be ridiculed; one would be revered—forever.

After an intense and heated conversation and multiple failed rock-paper-scissors attempts to decide the matter, we compromised: both of us would engage in the attack simultaneously in a banzai charge to win the game. With this solution in place, we began the crucial countdown to our highly synchronized attack. "5…4…3…2…1…*GO!*"

As soon as I came up over the rim of the ditch, I forgot that I had a teammate with whom I was going to share the glory. I ran as purely and purposefully as the attacking British at Gallipoli. As we ran, we began screaming some kind of rebel yell, and the excitement and fear of that moment made my heart race wildly and the pitch of my shrieks rise several octaves. Profound images of grandeur continued to flash through my mind as we rounded a turn in the road and ran screaming into the middle of a startled Boy Scout troop who were in the middle of setting up their tents!

They stared at us with eyes wide and mouths agape.

We tried to stop our raucous charge, but we couldn't do it without an awkward Frankenstein stagger. Our once hearty hollering petered out like deflating bagpipes, and I can only imagine how ridiculous we looked—covered in mud and lurching like drunken sailors. And, since there was nowhere to hide or any way to make a gracious exit, we were forced to pretend that nothing was wrong. We gave the still stunned group a halfhearted wave and tried to walk toward our campsite with as much nonchalance as we could muster, while the Scouts continued to stare speechlessly until we disappeared from sight.

My teammate and I walked along in silent confusion over what had just happened. As we approached our own campsites, the shouts and laughter of our classmates released our feelings of loss and washed over us as our footsteps became more and more leaden with disappointment and dread. We had blown our chance to become legends, and would have to face the ridicule of our peers.

As it turned out, the game had been won by one of the teams nearly twenty minutes before my teammate and I left the ditch and made our infamous charge! Because no one knew we were missing, everyone had returned to the campsite to retell stories of the game's heroic acts and to revel in the win that had just taken place. When the two of us came up to the fire pit, still muddy from head to toe, our classmates looked at us with as much befuddlement as the Boy Scouts we had just embarrassed ourselves in front of. We desperately wanted to tell them about our exploits and the way we had made it successfully around the game without being detected, but we needed even more desperately to take showers and wash off the filth. Unfortunately, we knew that, by the time we were done getting cleaned up, the entire celebration would be over.

So, after grabbing our clean clothes, towels, and soap, we headed off to the showers, a silent and somber procession of two, all too aware that we had just missed what felt like our one and only chance to share a fragile moment of greatness.

But I digress...

The Masks

● ● ● ● ●

My high school was so small, we could only field a few sports teams. We had boys' soccer, girls' volleyball, and boys' basketball—that was it! And with so few students, we struggled to fill those teams enough to compete against the other independent schools in the Buffalo area. If you had a pulse and could get a note from your doctor with a healthy endorsement, you could play; it didn't matter if you were a freshman, an exchange student from Germany or China, or suffered from asthma, Type II diabetes, or even a mild case of hemophilia. If we were going to have enough players to play the games, we needed everyone to play.

I started playing on the Cal soccer team as a freshman. We had no practice field, but our school was across the street from a huge city park, so we practiced there. There wasn't a soccer field in the park, so we used an unleveled patch of grass and some green metal trash cans as goalposts. Despite these conditions, our enthusiasm was high even if our skill levels were not. Playing on the soccer team at Cal became one of those cherished memories whose weight I can still feel today.

Having never played soccer before, I was put on defense. Because I did everything in my power to not let anyone get past me and score a goal, I was a natural fullback. I enjoyed staying back and then rushing forward to confront the other teams' offensive attempts to score. We had a good goalie who, although he suffered from hemophilia, was absolutely fearless. During my first season, however, he was injured, and the seriousness of his condition forced him to stop playing. His place was taken by another upperclassman who showed some promise, and we ended our season with quite a few wins. I finished out that year as a dependable fullback who was good, but certainly not great.

At the beginning of the next season, an injury to our starting goalie during a game forced me into the net. I showed enough promise that I became the team's regular goalie. I loved the jumping, the blocking, and the kicking that the position offered, and, like most of the rest of the team, my enthusiasm overwhelmed my innate lack of ability. With more practice and more games under my belt, my confidence started to grow. We had a couple of players who could score goals, and, as I got better at keeping the ball out of the net, we actually won a few games that year. I ended the season as an honorable mention to the all-star team of our tiny independent school division.

During the next season, however, everything changed. My skills as goalie continued to improve, but we had graduated or transferred out all of our top goal scorers. So even though I was making a lot of saves, we didn't have enough offensive power to put any points up on the board. We lost a lot of close games that year, but it didn't seem to matter to any of us players. The soccer team remained an extremely enthusiastic bunch who played each and every game with heart and effort. Through all the losses, we were a close-knit group who supported each other, no matter what. We might be losing, but we had fun playing and never once lacked team spirit!

It was just before a game with our hated rival, West Seneca Christian Academy, that this spirit spilled over and created a memorable event. Someone had the idea that the soccer players needed handdrawn Crayola-marker masks on our faces for the game. These markers seemed perfect for this. After all, they were water-based, which made cleanup a snap, and their vibrant colors seemed to really stand out on skin. The soccer team lined up to let several artistic girls from our class draw a ferocious game face on each of us. By the time the team boarded the bus to go to the game that afternoon, we all had facial tattoos that would have made the Maoris jealous.

During the bus ride to the game, we quickly found out that there is something truthful behind the psychology of masks. While we usually chattered like monkeys on the way to a game, this time there was a pensive and collective sense of preparation for some kind of battle.

When we arrived and started running laps around the field, we noticed that our appearances were having an impact on the other team. Although they rolled their eyes and snickered at us when they first saw our faces, our opponents seemed unsure about what to do with us and our newfound focus as we warmed up. And, as soon as the game began, it was obvious that we'd all been somehow transformed by the masks. We played with a sense of confidence and aggressiveness that we'd never had before. We were attacking and defending with a new fearlessness and vigor, and we were giving the other team a real run for their money. The result of this was clear: although we were playing against a team with far superior skills, the game was tied at the midway mark.

During halftime, we started to get the first indications that our Crayola facial decorations might not have been the smartest thing to do. As we went over to the bench to drink water and get our coach's strategy, it was evident that our masks were not as fresh as they'd been at the beginning of the game. The perspiration that had started to run down our faces was causing the colors to bleed, and our masks were now either dripping from our chins and onto our uniforms or were smudged abominations all over our faces. But this didn't seem to deter the magic that they seemed to hold over us, and we started the second half with the same sense of urgency and aggression, playing like the demons we now resembled.

Then it happened. Someone kicked the ball especially hard and it ricocheted right into the face of our main fullback, James. The impact not only shattered his glasses, but cut him and left him dazed on the ground. He was tended to by our concerned coaches and then driven right to the nearest hospital by a parent volunteer. We all watched him go, and although we didn't need any refocusing, the entire team turned its attention to winning the game for our wounded teammate. Although we fought tooth and nail to do this, we came up a little short, losing a hard-fought game by the score of three to two.

The bus ride home was particularly quiet because we were so full of mixed emotions. While we were all terribly concerned about James, we were also incredibly proud of ourselves for playing so hard against a tough opponent. In fact, we'd been so inspired by the power of the masks, someone recommended that we have them drawn on our faces for the rest of the games that season.

Once I got home, I made a series of phone calls to check on our fallen teammate. It turned out that he was fine, but the trip to the hospital had been a bit of an ordeal. As soon as he was wheeled into the building, the nurses and doctors saw the boy's discolored red-and-black face and rushed him straight into the emergency room, convinced that he had severe facial bone and muscle damage. The panic was so intense and their reactions so strong, the parent volunteer wasn't able to explain the reason behind his appearance, and the medical staff set about prepping the boy for immediate emergency surgery. When they'd gently washed off enough of the Crayola mask, they were finally able to see that he only had a few small cuts on his face and no ocular damage. They stitched him up and sent him on his way. However, their initial panic had caused such a stir that many of the staff around the emergency room were still noticeably shaken when James walked out of the hospital.

Upon hearing this good news, I went to take a post-game shower. I was tired and dirty, and I wanted to wash off the remnants of my green-and-black mask. The warm water refreshed my tired muscles, and as I stepped out and grabbed a towel, I enjoyed that satisfying feeling of fatigue that only comes from competing in athletics. I nonchalantly wiped the steamy bathroom mirror to look at myself, but the face that looked back at me had a jaundiced greenish tint to it. I shrieked and started scrubbing my face again at the sink. After I had done this several times without success, I ran to the phone to call my friend and teammate, Paolo.

"Um, hey, Paolo. How's it going?"

"Um, good, I guess."

"Yeah, well, I'm calling because I've taken a shower and washed my face like three times, and I still look like the Incredible Hulk!"

"I know! I've showered three times and I can't wash this red marker off my face! I don't know what I'm going to do! No matter what, the ink won't come off! It's faded to a pink color, so now I look like a cooked shrimp! I don't want to go outside or go to school looking like this!"

"Uh-huh, me neither. I'm going to keep trying until it washes off—or my skin comes off!"

There was a silence on the other end.

"Hey, Pete?"

"Yeah?"

"Let's never paint our faces with Crayola markers again, okay?"

"Okay."

And we didn't. And the Calasanctius soccer team lost each and every game it played that year.

But I digress…

The Fight

● ● ● ● ●

Paolo lived on the north side of Buffalo in a peaceful residential neighborhood that resembled a suburban development, and visiting him was usually a treat. We'd ride our bikes on the deserted streets and play outdoors in the serene surroundings, and it was blissful and idyllic. There was far less traffic and danger than in my neighborhood, so I always looked forward to sleepovers at his house.

During one of these, we went to a nearby store at the shopping plaza and purchased a pair of balsa-wood gliders. We were excited to get back to Paolo's house to assemble and fly them around the large front yard. With these iconic gliders, you can adjust the way the plane flies by moving the wings forward or backward in the slot of the fuselage. Bring them forward, the plane flies up in the air. Push them back, and it wants to dive. Set them askew, and the plane does a barrel roll. As we hightailed it back to Paolo's house, we each had our own ideas of what we were going to do with our gliders until they invariably got broken or stuck in a tree.

We were having such a great time playing with our gliders, we lost track of where we were and the passage of time. Looking back, I'm sure that I saw the paperboy and his assistant approaching at some point. But since I was having so much fun, my brain did not register them as any kind of threat. In fact, I didn't notice them until they were right at the end of the driveway looking at us with scornful faces. Actually, it took me a moment or two to realize that the paperboy was throwing insults at us by saying nasty things about our ages, our sexual orientation, and our mothers.

Paolo made a valiant attempt to usher me inside, but I wasn't going to let this knucklehead berate us that way. Instead of beating a hasty retreat, I walked forward into the fray. It wasn't until I was past the point of no return that I became aware that the paperboy was a little bigger than me and his friend was a giant man-child who towered over both Paolo and me.

Paolo was one of those unfortunate kids who was a late bloomer. While the rest of the boys in our grade sprouted mold-like mustaches on our upper lips and developed the lean and muscled physiques of young men, his body seemed doggedly determined to resist any growth at all. With his bambino physique, Paolo was the kid who found solace in the fact that he could play slot receiver in playground football games and be the tiny target who could avoid being hit during the epic dodgeball tournaments in gym class. But he rued the fact that he'd already gained the regrettable moniker of "little" before his name. The funny thing is that, a few years after this story took place, and during the summer of his sixteenth year, Paolo returned from his summer trip to Italy two inches *taller* than me. But on the day that the paperboy and his friend confronted us, Paolo was so short, he had to crane his neck to look at our opponents.

The paperboy and I started circling like sharks as he continued spouting insults at us and our glider flying. I, ever the fool, decided that I was going to stand up to him. When he bumped into me to show his dominance, I returned the awkward shoulder thump. For a moment, it seemed he was going to be content with this level of physicality, like two rams butting each other, and we continued to run into one another while his motor-mouth rumbled on.

Then, suddenly, he said quite clearly, "If you touch me again, I'm gonna knock your head off!"

I disregarded his threat and threw my shoulder into him again. This action is the last clear memory I have because after that, everything went white in a series of flashes. When my vision returned, I found myself face-down on the ground with the paperboy sitting on my back and his hands clutching a shock of my hair. I heard him command, "Say you give up."

Before I had a chance to answer, he knocked my face right onto the concrete driveway with an audible *thunk*. When he repeated his request and smashed my head down again, I didn't have to be asked again. I quickly told him that, in fact, I did give up. He got off me and I stood up. My head was ringing and dizziness fogged my vision, but I could see that poor Paolo was being easily restrained by the gigantic helper, but he was unharmed.

As the paperboy and his thug friend made fun of me and laughed at me, I actually grinned at the humor of their ridicule. In response, they gave me their angriest looks, and it made me wonder if I'd been concussed during the fight. To have been bloodied by a bully and then smile at his mean-spirited jokes didn't seem quite right, but I was too dazed to focus on this thought.

The paperboy and his giant friend finally got bored with us, and they walked off to continue their route. I had some good concrete burns oozing blood on my wrist and forehead, so Paolo rushed me inside for some first aid. And as his mom washed my wounds, put antibiotic cream on them, and covered them with well-placed Band-Aids, she threatened to go right out and track down those two boys and make them apologize to me. Paolo and I were nearly frantic in our attempts to keep her from doing this: somehow the image of the elegant Italian radiologist chasing after those two thugs with such a polite request would only add another layer to what already seemed like a bottomless pit of humiliation. She finally relented and let the aggressors disappear without retribution.

And in the midst of my throbbing wounds and the subtle quivering of my body, I was able to comprehend the fact that I had just had my ass kicked for the first time in my life.

Within a day or two, the road rash dried up and scabbed over, but my left eye swelled into a prototypical shiner that was such an ugly mixture of black and purple, it was like a neon sign advertising that I had been on the losing side of a fistfight. Because my dad's church was in a rougher neighborhood on the West Side, his parishioners all had a similar reaction when they saw me the following Sunday: "Oh, I bet the other guy's face looks worse, huh?"

But the fact was, I wasn't even sure that I had thrown a punch in the melee. I thought I had, but the white flashes had happened so quickly, I didn't know for sure. And it was pretty darn clear that if I *had* thrown any punches, they sure hadn't landed. As I awkwardly reported this to the supportive parishioners, their expressions went from sympathetic and proud to pitying and embarrassed, which only fed my own ebbing self-confidence. After all, having your ass kicked was shameful enough, but having an entire community of elderly church-goers suddenly realize it was almost too much for a teenage boy to bear.

That's why, when my parents went to Sears for something they needed, I insisted they buy me a weight set and bench press to put in the basement. I guess the plan was to work out until I was buff enough to take on the paperboy and redeem myself. As I proudly set up the bench in the musty and cluttered basement room and quickly read the short manual about the various arm, chest, and stomach exercises I could do, I envisioned punching that paperboy's face until it was bloody. The sand-filled plastic weights were perfect for me to work out with, and for quite a while, I religiously visited the basement and tried to grow muscles on my lean body. But, over time, I began to lose focus, and the workout sessions became less and less frequent. Finally, the weight bench became a storage area to keep boxes of family possessions off the damp floor. Yet every time I went over to Paolo's house—throughout the rest of high school and well into college—I looked around for that paperboy. I wanted nothing more than just one more opportunity to confront him and his thug to erase the shame from the fight. But I never saw him again.

That was the one and only fistfight I was personally involved in my entire life. Over the years, I saw my share of other people's fights, but I was never dragged into them. So, that first and only fight had deeper lessons for me that continued to influence me long after the physical scars faded and disappeared. Even today, I can still hear the final threat from that paperboy, and I can remember the consequences that followed my disregarding that threat. In that instant, I learned that threats are not always idle. When the dog is growling, the snake is rattling, the bees are buzzing, the baby is gagging, or the paperboy is saying that he's going to knock your head off, it's better to take these threats seriously. If you don't, you may end up with a guy sitting on your back and pounding your head into the pavement.

But I digress...

The Challenge

● ● ● ● ●

Shortly after the infamous ass-kicking at the hands of the paperboy, I failed yet another test of my manhood from none other than a boy named Marco. From the very first moment he walked through the doors of Calasanctius as a new student, it was evident that Marco was something unique. For starters, he was one of the best and purest athletes I've ever met in my life. Also, because he was Sicilian by blood, his dark skin, black curly hair, and muscular body made all the rest of us boys feel like we were nothing but pasty white weaklings. So when Marco wasn't making himself instantly popular with the girls and the other guys of the school with his handsome features and happy, infectious laugh, he was throwing a football farther, running faster, shooting more baskets, and playing any sport better than the rest of us. Oh—and for some reason, he hated me.

Looking back, I have no recollection as to why we got off on the wrong foot, but we did. As he formed a little gang of the other boys in my class who began to control the playground games at recess, he and his cronies sneered at me with displeasure. It seemed there was nothing I could do to resurrect my relationship with Marco and his horde, so it came as no real surprise when I finally received a passed note during class that said that he'd had enough of me and was challenging me to a fight in the boys' locker room after school that day.

Although I had been working out in the basement with the Sears weight set, I knew that it would be beyond stupid to go head-to-head with Marco. I knew that if I fought him, they'd be picking scraps of me off that dirty tiled floor for weeks to come. After all, he had bulging muscles and that vertical vein running down his biceps, which established his god-like status like Mars or Hercules. And as for me…well, I had demonstrated my pugilistic prowess in the fight with the paperboy.

My momma didn't raise no dummy. So, after school on the day of the scheduled fight, I bypassed the stairs that led down to the boys' locker room and headed *up*stairs to the school library. With Paolo once again as my wingman, we went in search of safety with the books and hid among the shelves. I figured that, when I didn't show up in the locker room for the fight, the gang would eventually lose interest and go home. Any shame I felt about this cowardly act was neutralized by the imagined physical pain I was sure Marco would inflict on me. After all, emotional wounds are easy to live with, cuts and bruises aren't.

And for a while it seemed that my plan had worked. The dreaded time of the fight came and went, and the silence of the library was comforting as Paolo and I pretended to be doing research for a nonexistent school project. But when I spotted Marco's henchmen scouring the hallways outside the library, obviously looking for me, I knew the jig was up. As Marco himself strutted into the room like the dominant male lion of a pride, his buddies spread out to cover the exits and prevent my escape

Marco wasn't just an intimidating figure to *me*; he'd told all of us numerous stories about his street fights in his old neighborhood, so every motion and gesture he made as he walked up to me that day proclaimed that I was doomed. He had the stone-faced expression of a confident warrior headed into a battle he knew he was going to win, and I looked like a startled small mammal whose hiding place had just been unearthed.

Marco looked around and said nonchalantly, "Did you get the message that I wanted to fight you in the boys' locker room after school?"

I shrugged my shoulders. "Uh-huh, I did."

"Well, what are you doing up here, then?"

His henchman Freddie snickered at me and began clucking like chicken. He hissed in contempt, "He's hiding up here!"

Marco moved his head slowly to look at me. "Is that true? Are you *hiding* up here?"

I figured that, at this point in the whole debacle, there was little point in lying, so I shrugged again and said, "Yep, I sure am."

"So, you're *scared* to fight me, huh?" he asked, and the other boys tittered and kept making chicken sounds at me.

"Yes I am, Marco. You'd pulverize me. And I don't want to fight you. I've never had a problem with you, but for some reason you hate me. I mean, I don't dislike you. So I headed up here to hide from you."

The other boys continued to deride me, but Marco suddenly shushed them. He looked back at me and his face almost had a warm smile on it when he said, "Okay, that's cool."

With no other comment, Marco turned and walked out of the library. His henchmen were almost too surprised to know what to do next, but they fell in line and followed him out. Paolo and I exhaled with relief, but we lingered in the library to avoid being ambushed in the hallway or outside the building in case it was some kind of trick. By the time we made our way outside, however, the school campus was empty and we walked on home.

From that moment on, Marco and I became the best of friends. For the next two years, until he transferred to a new school, we never mentioned the fight incident without smiling and laughing about it. If he thought any less of me for hiding from him in the library, he never showed it. In fact, he became one of the most important buddies I had during my early teen years. I'd like to think that my honesty about being scared actually defused the situation. I can't say what would have happened if I had pretended not to be scared, except that I would have had another ass-kicking to deal with, and I didn't need any more of those. So the lesson learned that day was that sometimes the truth *can* set you free.

But I digress...

Tim

There was an honored tradition at Calasanctius during those years that was called the Turkey Bowl. In this unofficial and unsanctioned tackle football game, the freshmen and sophomores competed against the juniors and seniors just before the Thanksgiving break. It was not condoned in any way by the school, but the game was such a huge source of pride among the students that it happened every year, regardless how many threats were made to stop it. The buildup to the game was almost feverish—captains were chosen by each team, training happened at recess and after school practices, and tensions in the hallways ran high as the members of the different classes met at their lockers and taunted one another.

Due to the sheer physical superiority of the older and larger upperclassmen, the outcome of the game was never in question; it was wholly expected and accepted that the freshmen and sophomores would get crushed. So when my team lost 70-0 during my freshman year, it wasn't a surprise. But the next year proved to be entirely different. Our team was led by none other than my pal Marco, and, as a class, we were a mix of good athletes and fierce competitors. There was a sense that, since we sophomores were the physical equals of many of the upperclassmen, we weren't going to be a pushover. And we weren't. We not only held our own, we started to dominate the game on both defense and offense. We eventually won, and the hard-fought upset victory instantly gave us a moment of glory that we, as teenage boys, so desperately sought.

When we became upperclassmen, the physical superiority of the juniors and seniors was reestablished again, and we easily won the next year's game. But during our senior year, the outcome of the game was in question again, due in part to a mass exodus of students leaving for other schools. This included Marco and some of the other more athletic boys, so our team of upperclassmen was more than a little depleted. Paolo and I were elected the captains, and it was our job to get the squad ready to take the final victory of our Turkey Bowl careers.

While we practiced enthusiastically and designed special trick plays, it was obvious that we lacked a clear advantage over the younger students. The inescapable truth was that our senior class was not only tiny in numbers, but half the boys seemed to be more into Lacoste shirts and Depeche Mode than playing tackle football. And as the game day approached, a desperation to win started to grow in the upperclassmen. After all, we'd been the authors of the disappointment of those classes we'd upset two years earlier, so we had an enhanced determination not to become victims ourselves to such a crushing defeat.

There was a new student at Calasanctius that year by the name of Tim. He was a pretty big kid, but his red-and-orange dyed hair, his choices in alternative music, and his rumored ambivalent sexual orientation made him someone who didn't appear to fit into our the rough and tumble world of us sport-playing boys. As a matter of fact, since he seemed to prefer chatting with the cool girls during recess, we even joked that he could help coordinate the cheerleaders for the big game! Meanwhile, even though our practices were revealing a team that was too stressed not to lose the game, we never once thought about including Tim in any of our Turkey Bowl preparations and practices.

However, a few days before the game, a whispered rumor floated through our tiny school like a cottonwood seed. According to a few credible sources, Tim had actually been the starting nose tackle on the varsity football team at the athletics-based traditional school he had attended before coming to Cal! He hadn't been accepted in that conservative environment, so he'd sought out a more inclusive and accepting school. Well, as soon as this news hit my ears, it was clear that we'd made a terrible mistake by excluding the guy, and that we needed him on our team to ensure the victory we were so desperate to get. So Paolo and I had the gall to walk right up to his lunch table, and without thinking about what we were doing, we invited him to join our Turkey Bowl team.

He looked up from his lunch and shook his head. "How come you haven't asked me before today?"

"We didn't know till now that you played nose tackle on a varsity team!"

"So, before you knew that, you didn't want me. But now that you know that stupid fact, you do, huh?"

We had no real answer to that except to shrug and say stupidly, "Uh, yeah."

"Yeah, well, no thanks."

The way that he started to eat his lunch again let us know that the conversation was over. We tried to interrupt him and begin begging, but he said, "You didn't want me until you knew that I could help you win. That isn't too cool, so I don't really want to play with you guys. And that's that."

We went away, but we were furious at him. We just couldn't believe that he'd reject us like that. It just confirmed what we already knew: he wasn't one of us. If he didn't care whether we upperclassmen lost the time-honored game, he was no friend of ours.

And I held onto that belief after we narrowly won the stupid football game and throughout the rest of that final year of high school. It wasn't until much later that I understood it had been *me* who was the ass that day. Ignoring Tim until we thought he could be useful to us made us the real losers. Human history is chock-full of such exploitation—of only giving a damn when something somehow impacts or improves your own selfish needs. And although I would love to say that I've never acted like that again, I know that I probably have. But my treatment of Tim made me painfully aware of how selfish and narrow-minded I can be at times, and I've strived to be a better person than that ever since.

But I digress...

"If I Were You, I'd Quit While I Was Ahead"

● ● ● ● ●

From September of 1992 until the end of April of 1993, my friend Ben, my dog Lou, and I hiked the entire length of the Appalachian Trail. We decided to start in Maine and do a southbound winter thru-hike because we figured that, if we could stay ahead of the worst weather, the off-seasons would be better for avoiding the critters and crowds of summer. Our judgment was wholly wrong, and we ended up not only facing blizzards, ice storms, and critters, we hiked through twice as many thru-hikers on the trail as most travelers do. But the experience, all two hundred and forty days of it, changed us as people and galvanized a friendship that continues to this day.

Hiking with a dog posed special problems. There were too many horror stories about insensitive dog owners who assumed that all the hikers on the trail were dog lovers, and I swore that I wouldn't be like that. I made sure to bring along a tent that I could set up if the shelters were full of people who didn't want a smelly or wet dog sharing their space, and I was quick to pitch it at the first sight of someone who might object to Lou. As the trail became more deserted during the winter, this aspect became less of an issue, and our little traveling squad was free to sleep wherever we wanted to.

There were two areas on the Appalachian Trail that were closed to dogs—Baxter State Park and the Great Smoky Mountains National Park. The only solution for this dilemma was to board Lou in a kennel and hike these areas without him. But from the first moments of planning our trip, I knew that I couldn't do that to him, and I made a plan to just skip hiking those two areas. Since we wouldn't be able to climb Mt. Katahdin in Baxter State Park, I proposed that Lou and I would walk the roads in from Millinocket, Maine, to make up for the prohibited section of trail. As for the Smoky Mountains portion, I similarly suggested that the dog and I would simply walk around the park and miss it altogether. To me, missing these sections of the AT was not as important as being with my dog, and I was happy to do it.

So that's what we did. Lou and I walked in from Millinocket, Maine, and met up with Ben after his ascent and descent of Mt. Katahdin. From Abol Bridge, we set off together on our way south, and we hiked together for the next six months. Along the way, we endured massive snowstorms that required the use of snowshoes, got frostbite and giardia, and came through the countless highs and lows of a great adventure. By the time we came to the northern boundary of the Great Smoky Mountains National Park, we were like an old married couple that had to split up and go separate ways. But I had an AAA map that loosely guided me on the roads around the park, and Ben was eager to forge ahead and cross the park on the AT, so we headed off away from one another.

As soon as Lou and I started down Interstate 40, some of the challenges ahead of us made themselves very clear. For starters, hiking along a busy highway was not like being on a solitary trail. Not only was negotiating the speeding traffic more dangerous, but finding available campsites in the populated areas was much harder. As we made our way onto the back roads that would take us through the towns of Cherokee and Bryson City, North Carolina, and finally on to Fontana Dam, where we would reunite with Ben, we were faced with the prospect of having to find somewhat public places to stop for the nights.

After spending our first evening in an off-season and abandoned RV campground, we got off the busier highway and onto a country road that snaked through the Piedmont farmland that surrounds the park. The rural environment made the road walking easier, but there were fewer and fewer available and open spaces to pitch a tent. So, as the sun started to get low in the sky and the weather seemed ready to start drizzling, I began to get a little desperate in our search for a place to camp. When we came to a compound of cottages on a hillside, I was audacious enough to stop a car that was leaving to ask about any possible camping nearby. The family in the car was just heading home from a weekend at their country camp, and they couldn't have been nicer to me. They pointed to a small wooded area by the side of the road up ahead where they thought no one would mind if I camped, as long as I didn't build a fire. They gave me a soda and a snack, and they also put their names and phone number on a piece of paper and gave it to me in case of emergency. As they drove away, Lou and I headed to the parcel of land they had suggested and began setting up the tent in the thicket of small trees.

I ate a quick dinner and got ready to hide in the tent. When I heard a vehicle go past, stop, and then back up, I tensed for a possible confrontation. I went outside and saw an elderly man sitting in a pickup truck that was idling down on the roadway. He smiled and greeted me with a hearty howdy. We went on to have a nice conversation. We talked about how the weather looked like it was changing, and I told him all about our thru-hike on the AT. When he finally drove away, he gave me such a big wave, I was no longer stressed about the possibility of being rousted. After all, between the young family at the camp and the older man in the truck, the people around this area seemed to be awfully nice.

The rain became heavier, and the sound of the big drops hitting the tent gently lulled me to sleep. I was warm and dry, and I slept soundly until Lou began barking and growling in the middle of the night. I was completely disoriented in the tent's darkness, but I quickly realized there was another dog outside the tent snarling at us, and that the entire copse of woods was being illuminated by spotlights. I tried to get my bearings, but the ferocious sounds of the dog and the squawking of radios was unsettling, and I struggled in vain to understand what the hell was happening.

A booming, authoritative voice took care of that: "You, in the tent, come on out, right now!"

I put a leash on Lou and went out into the rainy night. A handheld flashlight and a spotlight from a nearby sheriff's patrol car were pointed right at my eyes, blinding me so badly I could hardly make out how many people were around and where they were. While the barely restrained police K-9 continued to lunge and snap at us, the sheriff asked what I was doing camping there. I explained about the Appalachian Trail hike, the rule about no dogs in the Smoky Mountains, and my plan to walk around the park. He then asked tersely if I knew that I was on private property, and I responded that I did, in fact, but that I had obtained permission from a family to camp there.

The officer relayed this information to another man I couldn't see because of the lights, and this faceless voice responded that he'd like to know who it was that had given me permission. I told the sheriff that I had a piece of paper with the name and number on it, and that I could get it from the tent. He asked me to do just that, and once he had it in his hand, he went to his car to call the poor family in the middle of the night to verify my story. Without the sheriff's spotlight shining right into my eyes, I could now see the other man, who looked oddly familiar.

The sheriff came back up to the tent and reported that the family had indeed given me permission to sleep there, and the rest of my story checked out the same with them. The other man hemmed and hawed about camps being broken into recently and his concern that I would do the same thing. After I said that I only wanted a place to sleep for the night, the man proposed that I could stay, but was adamant that I needed to be on my way at sunrise. When the sheriff turned to me and asked if those conditions worked for me, I nodded.

But then, in a flash of recognition, I remembered where I'd seen the other man before—he was the elderly guy who had chatted with me from his truck earlier in the evening! I was now shaking from the confrontation with the sheriff and soaked through from the rain, and my anger began to well up toward this man.

The sheriff said confidently, "Well, I guess I'm all done here."

I nodded toward him, but then I pointed my finger right at the older man. "Okay, but I got a real question for you, sir! You stopped and talked with me earlier. How come you didn't ask me to leave then?"

The older man took a step back and said, "Well, it isn't my place to intervene with every stranger around these parts. I mean, I ain't the LAW!"

Anger made the volume of my voice rise too high. "But you're a MAN, aren't you? As a MAN, you could have asked me to keep on moving, right?"

Here the sheriff, with a North Carolina accent smooth as wet paint said to me, "If I were you, I'd quit while I was ahead."

I nodded, but I was too angry to stop at this point. "Yessir, but he saw me when it was still light out and the rain hadn't started falling. If he had talked to me about his concerns then, you wouldn't have been called in, that nice family wouldn't have been woken up in the middle of the night, and this whole ugly event could have been avoided! If he had only talked to me, then maybe we…"

"Like I said: If I were you, I would quit while I was ahead."

I wanted to argue some more, but there was something powerful in the sheriff's message that made me concede the point. I shook my head and said despondently, "Okay, okay. I'll be off this patch by sunrise."

After the men and their dog left, the dark woods got quiet again except for the raindrops falling from the leaves. My heart was still beating hard and my stomach burned with the anger I felt toward the old man. Eventually I did fall back to sleep, but I woke up with the sunrise and was under way before its rays hit the valley walls. I was still grumpy from the whole experience, and I walked with more purpose than usual for the first few miles of the day.

The rest of the walk around the national park was interesting but uneventful. That is, until I started walking the road in to Fontana Dam. Not only was the excitement over the impending reunion with Ben beginning to build, but I saw something funny. Near some dumpsters and bins in a big lot where the locals apparently disposed of their trash, I noticed the movement of shadowy critters running on the ground around them. I figured they were giant rats, and I grimaced at the thought of having to walk past these nasty rodents.

But as Lou and I got up close, it became clear that they weren't rats—they were puppies that someone had dropped off with their garbage. They scattered in fear as we approached, but luckily, they were drawn to Lou, and they came shyly back. I knew I couldn't leave them there, so I grabbed a nearby cardboard box and quickly put the entire litter of five inside it. I gave them water and some dog food, and when Lou and I resumed our trek toward Fontana Dam, I was carrying a box full of puppies.

By the time I made my way to the Fontana Dam Post Office and Store, I was really tired. When I told the ladies working in the store about finding the puppies at the garbage depot, I immediately received their guarded sympathies and the brilliant advice that, if I sat outside advertising free rescued puppies, people were bound to take them. Ben hadn't arrived yet, so I had the time to sit down next to the box of puppies and wait for prospective adopters to walk by.

While it was clear that the puppies were all from the same litter, there were two distinctly different-looking types. Three of them were totally adorable, with soft black and white fur and beautiful cinnamon eyes. The other two were wire-haired and a little more rough-looking. As they frolicked together in the bottom of the box, I wondered how the heck I was going to get rid of the less attractive ones. But, as people began to walk come by and ask about my box of puppies, the story of their discovery among the dumpsters touched their hearts and blinded their eyes so that they saw *all* the puppies as cute and cuddly and in need of rescue. It wasn't long before I had only one of each type left! As the ladies from the store closed up and locked the front door, one came over and said that she'd take those last two home with her. I didn't think it was possible, but somehow all five pups had found a new home in one afternoon!

Ben eventually showed up and we had an emotional reunion. As we walked to the nearby shelter to spend the night, we talked nonstop about our adventures apart from one another. There were several people already in the shelter, including an author who had come to interview hikers for a book she was writing about the trail. As a way of encouraging us to talk with her, she had brought beer—although this was against the park rules. As we cooked our dinners and drank our beers, a park ranger pulled up and came marching over to us with his index finger pointed at the contraband in our hands. He gruffly informed the author that he was well within his rights to write her up for the infraction, but then he apologized for being in such a bad mood. He went on to explain that it was because his wife had come home from work with two new puppies, and he was extremely unhappy with her for bringing two more mouths to feed.

It didn't take a rocket scientist to figure out that the ranger's wife was the woman at the store who'd taken those last two pups, and that *I* was the real source of the ranger's bad mood. And just as I started to confess this to him, I heard that wise sheriff's voice in my head: "If I were you, I'd quit while I was ahead."

I didn't say anything as I poured my beer out onto the ground, and I was okay with that.

But I digress...

The Three Most
Embarrassing Stories

● ● ● ● ●

While it's always tricky to decide which story is the second or third most embarrassing story of my life, the most embarrassing story is easy to choose—and it remains the undisputed champion!

The Farting Horse (Embarrassing Story #3)

When my parents and I moved to Buffalo in 1974, we came to a Rust-Belt city that was in full decline from its glory years. That being said, it was still stubbornly holding onto a few remnants of its much brighter past. For example, there were several architectural gems in the downtown, an amazing park system, sprawling neighborhoods of large turn-of-the-century manses, and several hallowed professional sports teams. There was also an indoor polo stadium—a holdover from the ritzy days of the 1920s—that had been turned into an indoor horse riding facility called Saddle & Bridle Club.

I don't know how or why my mother did it, but she signed me up for riding lessons at Saddle & Bridle. To an eight-year-old boy, horseback riding still had a certain romantic allure to it. Being a child of one of the last generations to run around playing cowboys and Indians, I can honestly say that I had given serious thought to becoming a cowboy when I grew up. Even when I found out that I would be riding English saddles instead of Western pom saddles, cantering around the ring instead of galloping across the open prairie, and being forced to wear the black velveteen crash helmets of the jumpers instead of Stetsons during my lessons at Saddle & Bridle, I didn't have the instant revulsion one would think. I guess I had a sense that, if I could learn the namby-pamby ways of English riding and jumping, I could easily transfer the general riding knowledge onto the open range when I got my first job as a cowpoke. That self-delusion eroded subtly with each year I took lessons there, until it was utterly uncool for a thirteen-year-old to be wearing a sissy helmet to go prancing around on a woman's saddle.

The Saddle & Bridle Club was a pretty incredible place. The main arena was a dirt-floored ring sheltered by a trussed roof nearly five stories overhead. Three of the four walls were made up almost entirely of windows, but over the decades, many of the square panes of glass had been broken and not replaced. This allowed in not only the coldness from the outside, but also a number of small song sparrows, and they flittered and scattered freely in the open space. Behind the imposing wooden wall of the polo ring, there were wooden bleachers and spectator boxes. There was even a space where the announcers had sat to broadcast the games over the intercoms. A thick dirty dust covered everything in the polo ring. The stables were arranged around the ring, and the whole space smelled and looked like a temple to the equestrian world.

The main impetus for my continuing to take riding lessons at Saddle & Bridle after it was clearly uncool was a horse named Blackie. I had ridden many of the horses, but I developed a special connection with this smaller black horse, mainly because he had a horrendous temper. Around humans, he was a sweet and gentle creature. But the instant another of his own kind got too close, he'd pin back his ears and try to kick and bite the intruder with vicious intent. For obvious reasons, these behaviors made him very unpopular with other riders—but when you're stuck in an enclosed arena with five to eight other horses, and you spend the entire hour going round and round the ring, it's a virtual certainty that you'll get close to one of them. The last thing anyone else wanted was to have to keep their horse from going ballistic each and every time this happened!

But I loved that horse. He wasn't the biggest or the faster, but he was the meanest, and that, to me, made him the coolest horse in the whole place. It got to the point that the guys working in the stables no longer had to ask who I wanted to ride that day—I would just come in and walk to his stall and start getting him ready for the lesson.

Riding Blackie during a lesson was definitely challenging, but that was the fun of it. I had to keep a close eye on the other horses and know where they were at all times, even if the entire group was cantering around at different speeds. And whenever those ears of his went back, it was time to head to a different part of the arena or start talking Blackie down. That the other riders gave us looks of displeasure only made the situation cooler, in my eyes: both Blackie and I were outsiders to the blue-blood culture that came to the club. We were the underdogs. And to a preteen boy, there was nothing better.

On the day of this story, however, when I got to the Saddle & Bridle Club and made my way to Blackie's stall as usual, he wasn't there. I went back to the office to ask where he was and was told that he'd been taken to the vet for his annual checkup and I'd have to ride another horse for that lesson. My shoulders dropped at the news—I only came to the place for the thrill of riding Blackie. I was in such a state of disappointment, I was unable to make a choice, so I was assigned Quevieve, an older thoroughbred-looking horse that was meek and mild. Grudgingly, I mounted up and started my lesson.

I rode around the arena listlessly because it was so boring. Quevieve got along with all the other horses, and his ears stayed up and forward the whole time. His mood seemed eager and upbeat, with none of the dark and dangerous qualities that I sought in a horse. But it didn't take long for me to notice that something was wrong with him that day. Although perky and upbeat, the horse began to make loud *THRTSS* sounds as he began releasing gas. Then some more. I don't know if you've ever been riding on a horse when it farts, but it has the volume of a backfiring rocket. I felt a surging sense of embarrassment as the horse continued to *THRTSS* noisily as we trotted around the ring. Not only was I trapped on top of such a benign and unsexy horse—which had already peppered my fragile self-confidence—but this glue-factory candidate began to pop out louder and louder farts: *THRTSS…THRTSS…**THRTSS!***

When we started to canter, the farts started to hurt Quevieve. Each new *THRTSS* was followed by a pained whinny and a mild buck. This, in turn, caused the old horse to break into a gallop, which caused more painful farts to come out faster and harder. Soon the entire arena was stopped and staring at the spectacle. ***THRTSS!*** WHINNY…BUCK.

I sensed that I was in enough trouble that holding onto the reins even tighter was advisable, but Quevieve turned into a bucking bronco. *THRTSS!* WHINNY…BUCK! The horse had started to leave the ground to kick out and spin until I could feel my thigh grip loosening. When this happened, my butt came way out of the saddle as Quevieve bucked high in the air and smacked down hard upon landing. I started to slide to the side, which, like the listing of a sinking of a ship, spelled my doom.

THRTSS! WHINNY…BUCK! *THRTSS!* WHINNY, *BUCK!*

Quevieve was now in full-blown rodeo mode. In the midst of a world that was whirling and twirling around, I remember my butt flying out of the saddle with no chance that it was going to land back on the horse. Everything slipped into super slow-motion as my body was thrown high in the air, and I watched the world turn upside down as I spun to the dirt floor of the arena. I landed with a thud, and looked up to see Quevieve still sprinting and bucking around the ring—***THRTSS!*** WHINNY, BUCK! *THRTSS!* WHINNY…BUCK! ***THRTSS!*** WHINNY, *BUCK!*

My mother still chuckles about the sight of me being helped up off the ground afterwards. My black velveteen hat had flown off somewhere, and when I stood up, my face was so pale it was like the shining alabaster of a full moon. My clothes and hair were full of manure and dirt, and my eyes swam in their sockets with shock. By this point, Quevieve had run out of gas, literally, and he was calming down in the corner. He may have been in nearly as much shock as I was over what had just happened.

As for me, I was standing in the center of the ring with my instructor and other people helping to brush off the dirt, and if there had been a hole I could have jumped into at that moment, I would have done so willingly! The attention of all the people during my embarrassing debacle…the shattering of all preconceived notions of my own ruggedness…well, what kind of cowboy allows an ancient farting horse to buck him off? Quevieve had taken me to what I thought was the nadir of embarrassment.

But I was wrong. The old adage that you have to get right back on the horse was held as the gospel truth at Saddle & Bridle, and now that it was clear that I had no broken bones or other physical wounds, I was expected to hop right back on Quevieve. I tried to decline the offer, but my teacher was quite firm on this—both the horse and the human needed to be reminded of who was in charge. So the horse was brought to the mounting platform and I was instructed to get back on his back. Because I was convinced that Quevieve was not, in fact, done with farting, I wanted to cleave the horse's head in two with an axe for the pain of the next round of humiliating gas-powered bronco riding I assumed was coming. But luckily, other than a few light sputters, Quevieve was done, and we finished the rest of the lesson without incident.

However, the irreparable damage was done. If I had been riding the horse on trails and had been far away from other people when the farting event had happened, I'd have forgotten and forgiven the whole thing. But the embarrassment of having the farting-horse experience in front of people was too much for me to handle. Even though I got to ride my beloved Blackie again during the next lessons, I soon quit going to them altogether.

The Shower Curtain Incident (Embarrassing Story #2)

As a junior at Bowdoin College, I shared an apartment with three of my friends in the infamous sixteen-story dormitory called The Tower. As incredible as it sounds, this building once had the distinction of being one of the tallest in all of Maine. Anyway, the layout of the building is extremely important to this story. The two elevators formed the core of the building. Around these, on each floor, there were four four-bedroom apartments. Each of these had two single bedrooms on either side of a common room, with a bathroom separating each apartment on the floor. The bathrooms between apartments housing different genders were locked to prevent any awkward mixing of the sexes.

One weekend afternoon, I decided to take a shower before dinner. My roommates, Paolo and Randy, were in the common room watching TV with my girlfriend, Shelly. I walked past them with my ditty bag, clean clothes, and a towel without any fanfare, and went into our bathroom.

I enjoyed the long hot shower, but when I reached outside the shower stall to get my towel from the hook I'd left it on, it was not there. No reason to panic—I just assumed it had fallen to the floor. I bent down to grope around for the missing towel, but it wasn't there either. I poked my head out around the shower curtain to see if it had somehow fallen farther away from my grasp. But it was nowhere to be seen—nor were my clothes on the sink counter anymore. Then I heard tittering coming from the common room, and I knew what had happened: I had just been punked by my friends!

I closed the shower curtain and tried to figure out how I could get around this prank. The grown-up version of me would have walked out of the bathroom naked as a jaybird, and the shock of such a bold move would have been more than enough to get me out of the situation. But the twenty-year-old me was in no place in his life to walk *anywhere* in the nude, so I stayed in the safety of the shower stall and tried to think of something clever to do. When my friends started to mock me from the other room, I grew desperate to come up with something that would let me beat them. But the fact was, there was not a stitch of clothing or any towels or even washcloths that I could cover myself up with to get out of the bathroom and back to my room. The only thing shielding my nakedness was a flimsy shower curtain.

Flash of brilliance: the shower curtain!

I unhooked the clips that held it to the rod and wrapped it around myself like a translucent toga. That was when I made the mistake I would later regret. If I had just walked out and faced the conspirators with my improvised covering, the embarrassment I was going to feel later would have been kept to a minimum. But I was so damn proud of my novel idea to use the shower curtain to outwit my friends, I decided to start talking smack before I came out. In a near yell, I announced that I had outsmarted them all and would soon demonstrate my superiority. I sashayed out with too much confidence and broke into an immature tirade about how they had thought they could beat me, but that I was the smartest one. As I juked my way past the common room, they all laughed at me, so I added a bouncy poem declaring that I was smart and they were dumb. It ended in a rousingly intelligent chorus of "Neener, neener!"

I was immensely proud of myself as I reached for the doorknob of my room. I had, after all, overcome this attempt to humiliate me. I couldn't wait to get inside to change into my clothes so that I could come back out and gloat over my victory. But the door to my room was locked. It didn't take much more than the initial touch to realize this, but I turned the knob several times before conceding the fact that my friends had locked me out. And then the ultimate wave of shame washed over me as I realized that I had to turn around and face the now hysterical group to beg for my key. From the greatest victory straight down to the most embarrassing defeat—all in a matter of seconds!

When I came to the conclusion that no psychic abilities, my anemic lock-picking skills, or a further embarrassing call to the building's security office would get me into my room, I made my way back toward the common room to face the humiliation. The crinkle of the shower curtain only made them laugh harder as I asked, "Can I please have my key?"

They all acted as though I'd said something incredibly funny, and then Paolo asked, "Are you having problems?"

"Yeah, I need my key. I can't get into my room."

"We're too *dumb* to have your key, right?"

"Come on, just give it to me."

"Only if you say that we're smart and you're dumb."

I looked at them and knew that, if I wanted to get out of this nightmare, I would have to eat my own words. I said softly, "You're smart and I'm dumb."

"Oh, I didn't hear that. You need to say it louder."

When I said it with more volume, Paolo cupped his hand around his ear and said, "Oh, I couldn't hear you. What did you say?"

This time I yelled as loud as I could, "You're smart and I'm dumb!!"

Their laughter was riotous as they handed the key to me.

In the privacy of my room, I realized that my entire body was clenched in embarrassment, and I swore that I wouldn't leave my room again till they'd all left the common room.

Of course, that didn't happen. As soon as it was dinnertime, I was hungry enough to grudgingly follow them to the dining hall and eat with them. I didn't have a healthy appetite that night, though, because I had eaten too much crow earlier, but all was soon forgiven. Forgiven, but never forgotten.

The prime life lesson I learned that day was to be very cautious before trash-talking. If I hadn't been so cocky and verbose as I walked out of the bathroom, my embarrassment would not have been nearly as bad.

Pooping My Pants (Embarrassing Story #1)

When I was a junior in college, my father took a year-long sabbatical from his Episcopal parish in Buffalo. After my parents toured the United States to reconnect with old friends and revisit some of the important places of their lives, they were set to fly over to Great Britain for an extended visit to England, Wales, Scotland, and Ireland. Dad had become very interested in Celtic influences in early Irish Christian history, and he was eager to tour religious sites and learn about this history firsthand. And because the beginning of their European trip coincided with the beginning of my college spring break, I was invited to go with them to London for a week of sightseeing.

Because they would be staying longer, my parents had rented a flat in the London neighborhood called Mayfair. As soon as the airport taxi dropped us off there, we noticed that the apartment was very close to a vibrant area with a wide variety of restaurants and shops. As a matter of fact, just down the street from us was a cluster of international restaurants, so we would be all set for dinners during our stay— we'd be supping on Indian, Italian, Lebanese, or Japanese cuisine.

After our first day of sightseeing in London, we decided to eat dinner at the Lebanese restaurant. We sat down in the warm, dark restaurant and were completely overwhelmed by the extensive menu the waiter handed to us. There were just far too many appetizers, salads, and entrées to choose from, and we had no idea how to pick just a few items and get the best food. My dad then had a brilliant idea, albeit one that reeked of being rich and ugly Americans, I guess. He told the waiter that, since we couldn't decide, we wanted him to order the food for our dinner as if we were members of his family. The waiter, obviously elated at the prospect of racking up a huge bill and securing a good tip, seemed hell-bent on getting as much delectable Lebanese food into our stomachs as they could humanly hold.

The food that came out was definitely in the top five meals of my life! The handmade hummus was tart, garlicky, and unbelievably delicious, and, on top of the freshly baked pita bread, it made us close our eyes in appreciation. The side dishes that followed were equally delicious—baba ghanoush, grape leaves, and couscous salad. When the main entrées came out, the lamb and other meats were succulent and seasoned with the most amazing spices. The Lebanese beers flowed, and the food was devoured as soon as it came out to us. A dessert of baklava and Lebanese coffee capped an evening that was perfect from beginning to end. We lumbered back to our flat completely sated, almost euphoric in having discovered the greatest way to order food at a new restaurant.

The next day, we went to the Tower of London and Parliament. While we enjoyed learning about the city's history, my parents were thrilled to eat ploughman's lunches in a pub. Not a fan of the pâtés that accompanied these, I was discovering the seductive power of drinking bitters with the noontime meal. Throughout that exciting day, our anticipation about having evening dinner in the Indian restaurant continued to build.

This restaurant was well-lit and very aromatic, and as we sat down, we did not even glance at the menus when they were handed to us. Instead, my father began his spiel and gave the waiter carte blanche to serve whatever he thought we would enjoy. And the man did not disappoint. As the delicious and different dishes kept coming out, they were marked by a growing level of spiciness. My dad and I threw caution to the wind and devoured everything put in front of us, regardless of how much it singed our esophagi or made sweat bead up on our foreheads. To combat the heat, we just tried to wash it away with multiple bottles of cold Kingfisher beer. Meanwhile, my mother wisely opted to eat the only innocent dish on the table, a curried okra entrée called bhindi masala. By the end of the meal, my dad and I had eaten all the food, and we even had room for a few Turkish Delights for dessert.

We returned to our flat smugly satisfied with ourselves again. We had, in fact, just proven that we now had the perfect way to order absolutely fantastic meals at all of the international restaurants in London. Even though my stomach felt like a nuclear reactor when I went to bed that night, I was still savoring the exotic dinner experience at the Indian restaurant, and the discomfort seemed an appropriate toll for such a sumptuous evening.

That all stopped when my guts signaled that they were ready to exit my body. It was still dark out when I awoke with the pure panic that I had to get to the bathroom *instantly*. When I got into the loo, however, I was faced with a conundrum. Now, if you have some doubt to as the real definition of a conundrum, let me enlighten you. While Webster's dictionary might have it as a problem with no clear solution, I would clarify that by saying that it actually means realizing that you're about to have a bout of explosive diarrhea simultaneous with the moment that you're going to vomit uncontrollably, and you must decide which one you're going to immediately address! With three nanoseconds to decide, I opted to puke in the wastebasket and squirt in the toilet.

With the first double-barreled barrage done, I cleaned up the best I could and made my way back toward my bed. Unfortunately, there was much more ammo left in me, and I threw up a Jackson Pollock painting on the floor of the apartment. By that time, my poor parents were awake and helping me as much as they could, and when this final bout was finished, I limped back to my bedroom and slept with the garbage can next to me, just in case.

I was so horribly sick the next day, we didn't venture out of the flat. And while my father enjoyed twenty-four hours apparently dodging the bullet, he fell victim to the same symptoms the very next night. It was clear that we had food poisoning, which we quickly named "Punjab Poisoning." My mother, because she'd stuck to the okra dish and skipped the other entrées, never got sick. At first, this seemed to be a good thing for her, but after having to help not one, but two, pukers convalesce, she lost some of her humor about her unpleasant role in the fiasco.

In the end, we lost two complete days of sightseeing. So, on the third day, we decided that we didn't have any more time to spare. Since my father and I seemed recovered enough to walk around, we headed out for Buckingham Palace. It was a beautiful spring day in London; the sun was shining and the streets were full of people—both native Londoners and tourists. My mom, my dad, and I watched the changing of the guards and took in the view of the palace from behind the fence and felt we had checked off one of the bigger items on our list of the sights we wanted to see.

But on the way back to the Tube, I made a critical mistake. I should have known better: when I felt the pang in my guts from gas pressure, I gently pushed. I mean, not without some self-diagnosis of my system—I carefully tested myself and pushed a little more and more until I was sure that I was fine. And, since we were outside with throngs of people nearby on the sidewalks, I thought that their noisy presence would mute the toot. When I was sure that nothing out of the ordinary was going to happen, I pushed a little more to force the fart out. But my body betrayed me, and more than just gas was passed!

I don't know if you've ever had the displeasure of soiling yourself, but it's an experience that cannot be aptly described. My suddenly soggy underwear took on that loathed feeling of a wet swimsuit, a most intolerably uncomfortable tactile sensation that still haunts me today. To combat this horrendous feeling, I started walking with my legs apart and my pelvis pushed forward. I thought I was being stealthy enough to avoid detection, but the booming voice of my father shattered that illusion.

[It is important for this story to know that, although my father was a born-and-bred Hoosier from the great state of Indiana, whenever I rethink this story or retell it, his voice has both the volume and twang of a loudmouth Texan oilman. I don't know why that is, but it is.]

"What's the matter, son? Why're you walking so funny?"

My father had been an Episcopal priest for much of his adult life, and he could project his voice to fill any cavernous sanctuary or space. His question, albeit based on parental concern for me, had enough volume that I was sure most of the citizens of London were now staring at me and my poopy underwear. I continued walking along like a saddle-sore cowboy and just muttered quietly, "Nothing, Dad. Let's just keep walking."

But he was not to be deterred. His voice boomed out again to repeat his question: "What's the matter, son? Why are you walking so funny?"

I cringed and tried to look for a place to hide. I turned toward him and whispered loudly, "I'm fine, Dad. Let's just keep walking."

"Well, you aren't walking like you're fine. Are you in pain? Is that why you're walking so funny?"

I was now thoroughly convinced that the entire population of Great Britain was aware of my situation, and my face turned crimson as I slowed and got closer to my dad to give him some kind of explanation. The crowded sidewalk and my loaded underwear did not make this maneuver an easy one, but I got close to him and leaned in—two silent gestures I hoped my father would take as less-than-subtle hints that I was going to say something I didn't want shared with the thousands of other people near me.

I attempted to explain the situation. "Shh, Dad. I thought I had to fart, but I pooped my pants."

My father's face seemed not to register what I had just said. He shook his head and acted genuinely confused. "*What?*"

I whispered more harshly, "Dad, I tried to fart, but I pooped my pants. I'm walking this way because my underwear's soiled!"

My father reared back and exclaimed, "Did you just say you pooped your pants?"

"Shhh! Jesus, Dad, yes, I did!"

My father amped his volume up to the proverbial "11" and turned toward my mother. "Oh my God, he POOPED his pants!!"

With that, I felt as though the very atmosphere of the planet came crashing down upon me. As a matter of fact, at that very moment—as a food-poisoned twenty-year-old with an underwear full of poop—I *begged* for something to fall from the sky and crush me into a powder that would blow away with the merest of winds. But nothing did, and I was forced to continue walking with that ridiculous gait while my face burned with shame. I hadn't heard anyone laughing at my father's comment, but in my head was a deafening cacophony of scornful laughter that was focused on me and my poopy pants. I was so angry, I quit walking funny and instead marched home with the purposeful gait of someone who has just lived through the most embarrassing moment of his life.

But I digress...

"Want to Know What They Do to Boys Like You in Prison?"

● ● ● ● ●

During the summer of 1989, I embarked on a grand adventure. I had spent the previous year working on various commercial fishing boats on the East Coast, but the big rumor on the decks of those boats was that the *real* money was made fishing in Alaska. So, after doing some research, I found out that most of the companies that had fishing boats up there could be found in the city of Seattle, and I set off for that city to strike it rich. I took the train from Buffalo to Seattle with no solid plans beyond just getting there and asking around the docks. Ah, to have the confidence of youth again!

Once I landed in Seattle, I bought a newspaper to see if there were any Alaskan fishing jobs listed in the classifieds. There were. So I took a city bus to the office of one of the companies that was advertising work on processing ships, and I got myself a job. The fact that I was drug-free and had some experience on the decks of fishing boats made me a viable candidate, and my job search was over just a few hours after it started.

I wasn't required to be at the Sea-Tac airport to fly up to my new job for nearly a week, so I had ample time to explore Seattle. The only person I knew in the city was an obscure niece of a friend of a friend of my mother's, but when I called her to ask for some tips on sightseeing destinations, this young woman and her family invited me to move out of my seedy hotel room and right into their home. The next seven days were some of the most blissful of my life as I tried to cram in everything I knew I wouldn't be able to do during the next few months of hard labor on board a ship in the Aleutian Islands.

When it came time to travel up to Dutch Harbor with the other new hires, each step in the process was a clear indication that I was leaving my normal life and going to a fantastical and otherworldly place. When we boarded the Boeing 737 to fly from Anchorage to Dutch Harbor, there was no doubt that this final leg of the trip was an intense metaphor for what awaited me in the Bering Sea. Each and every person around me was a rugged and larger-than-life individual involved in the fishing industry. To call them a rough-and-tumble crowd would be an understatement.

At first, the flight was nondescript—just your typical commercial airplane trip. But when the captain came on the intercom to announce our approach into Dutch, I noticed many of the passengers grip their armrests with some force. Their involuntary response made me stiffen up with my own dread of what was coming, though I didn't yet know what that was.

When we dipped below the ever-present overcast of the place, I could see just how insanely beautiful Dutch Harbor and the Aleutian Islands are. Down below us, the landscape was breathtaking. There was an Ireland-like greenness, a rugged and inhospitable coastline, an enormous volcanic mountain, and a sprawling fishing harbor. And as the plane suddenly banked hard, I could see that the Dutch Harbor airport was tucked into a small patch of land between the mountainside and the open water of the harbor. Clearly, there was no margin for error for landing or taking off from the single runway, and when the plane dropped like it was going to pin itself to the pavement, I gripped the armrests with the understanding that we were, very possibly, going to die. I'd never closed my eyes before on an airplane flight, but I did on this one. As soon as the tires *whumped* down onto the runway, the brakes were applied so hard that our seats were pushed forward. All of us passengers uttered a collective groan that only ceased when the plane came to a safe and complete stop, at which point the groan transformed into a deep sigh of relief.

After a night in a hotel comprised of trailers welded together, all the new hires were driven down to the docks. As we pulled up to the *Spindrift*, the ship that we would call home for the next four months, we put down our bags and instantly joined the rest of the crew in unloading the catch of over a half million pounds of frozen Atka mackerel directly onto a Japanese freighter. The ancient processing ship *Spindrift* was a 180-foot-long former factory trawler, and she not only had the rugged appearance of a tried-and-true working vessel, she looked like some kind of prison ship. She had a crew of forty people, and I quickly found myself in the midst of an odd collection of genders, ethnicities, and languages that was only bridged by the communal desire to make as much money as possible.

The *Spindrift* no longer fished for itself, but instead used two smaller catcher boats that dragged their nets to supply the "mother ship" with fish. The deckhands were responsible for winching aboard the full "bags" from the catcher boats and emptying them into the holds for processing. These nets were the size of school buses, so the process was something to behold. Not that I saw much of it during my first few weeks on board. I'd been hired as a plain processor, so I worked on the line in the bowels of the ship and rarely saw a glimpse of the sun. I lived in the bow bunkroom with two Mexican migrant farm workers, a schizophrenic boy, a drunk, another young kid, and a couple of ex-cons fresh from prison. And because of the bunkroom's location in the bow of the ship, whenever the weather turned and got rough, our bedroom bucked like a bronco, and water shot up the hawser pipes like geysers just outside our room.

When there was an opening for a deckhand, I was offered the position. It was a small promotion that resulted in my getting to sleep in a better bunkroom and being able to work outside whenever it was time to winch and unload the nets into the hold. During those days when we were fishing, our normal work shifts were sixteen and a half hours long, and thanks to the hand-drawn graph in the galley—which was updated daily to show how much fish was processed that day and the resulting income for each crew member—there was the clearest connection between work effort and income that I've ever had in my life. This lure of making money motivated even the laziest workers to push through their fatigue and work, work, work.

Since the *Spindrift* was a floating village with an entire community of personalities that lived, loved, and processed over the course of that summer, it is important to this story to highlight some of the crew and some of the events that led up to the final violent confrontation. This means skipping a lot of other stories, but that's the way it has to be sometimes.

Each of the three shifts had a foreman. This was usually just another crewman who was responsible for assembling the best shift rosters and leading by example. It was his role to keep all of us cutting as quickly as we could and to remind us that the more we worked, the more money we made. When I became a deckhand, my deck boss became my supervisor. I cannot remember his real name anymore, but I called him Pa. He was an army veteran with long hair, tattoos up and down his arms, and a warm smile, and he kept me safe and happy throughout my time on the deck. He was good-natured and had a quick sense of humor, but he took real pride in making us deckhands the best that we could be.

A rumor began to circulate among the cutters that an infamous former foreman was returning to the *Spindrift*, and this had everyone a-titter with nervousness. His name was Earl, and he was rumored to be a giant of a man who had not only spent time at San Quentin and Folsom prisons, but had supposedly had his front teeth knocked out and his nose ripped off in a fight. Those who knew Earl spoke of him with a quiet reverence that bordered on fear, and the rumor was that, after making a wheelbarrow-full of cash during the last pollock roe season, he'd spent everything he'd made on buying drugs until he was found wandering the streets of Seattle in his underwear. Somehow, he'd been rehired to work on the *Spindrift*, and the rumor was that he was on his way.

When Earl finally came aboard, it was easy to see that many of the stories were true. He *was* a giant—nearly four inches taller than me and nearly double my weight—with red hair that wrapped around his head like flame. His life had been as tumultuous as advertised. He and his gang had enjoyed a lucrative career "rolling" gay men in San Francisco, but their life of crime had brought them into direct contact with a notoriously vicious Mexican gang. In a violent dispute over territory, this rival gang had, indeed, smashed Earl's face with a pipe, ripped off his nose, and shattered his front teeth. After he got out of the hospital, he had gotten some kind of revenge, but he never said what that was, exactly. He only inferred that it was violent enough to land him in San Quentin…again.

From the moment he stepped aboard the ship, the rest of the crew kept watchful eyes on Earl, and we all knew where he was at all times. If he was the shark, we were the minnows. Which makes the fact that I decided to play a practical joke on Earl even more startling.

We were steaming toward port and had nothing to do until it was time to unload the ship, so most of the crew came up on deck to take in the sunshine. As we enjoyed this brief period of idleness in the good weather, I noticed that Earl was falling asleep atop a pair of big steel fishing "doors" that were stored there. The man always wore Sorel winter boots, and he never tied them, so I came up quietly to the slumbering giant and tied his laces together. Everyone saw me do this, and their expressions were a mixture of amusement and fear. When Earl woke up and tried to stand, he stumbled forward and almost fell face-down on the deck. He scanned the crowd menacingly before asking who had done this to him. I jokingly told him that a kid in the crew had, but his expression toward Ozzie was so violent and hateful that I admitted to the deed—and prepped myself to get beaten to a pulp. I was shocked when Earl began to grin warmly—he thought the whole thing was funny, and he took me under his wing as though I was a member of his family.

The source of the upcoming trouble was a woman by the name of Cheryl. Although she was the daughter of a librarian and one of the best-read people I've ever met, she also slept with a lot of the guys. She dated Pa for a while, but then they broke up and she started dating the engineer. When they broke up, she turned her attention on a skinny kid named Tommy. Cheryl seemed to want something more than just sex from Tommy, which caused their relationship to develop slower than usual. And while it was almost touching to see this romance grow in such a stark and desperate environment, the slow pace created a simmering tension among the other crew members who were lining up for their turns with Cheryl. Pretty soon, the whole situation was only one spark away from combusting.

By October, we had come to the end of the summer season. We had finished up fishing for Atka mackerel and had switched over to sole without much success. We all knew that, at any moment, the company might decide it was time to steam back to Seattle and prepare the boat for the lucrative winter season. As soon as that decision was made, we were going home.

We headed into Dutch Harbor to pick up a new captain. Our current captain's contract was up, so once the boat was ready to fish again, a new leader would be coming aboard to guide us for the rest of the season. But as soon as we docked, we were told that the new captain's flight had been terribly delayed, and we were forced to wait until he arrived. The restless crew realized that this was the perfect opportunity to sneak off the boat to buy booze, and soon word went around that there was going to be a party in the women's bunkroom. This space was across the hallway from the deckhand's bunkroom, at the base of the stairs to the wheelhouse. But despite this overly central location, it was the chosen site of the night's festivities.

I made one of the smartest decisions of my life by opting not to have anything to do with the whole event. It was so obvious to me and another deckhand named Dennis that this party was only going to end in disaster, we resisted all the urgings of our fellow crewmembers and chose to spend the night safely in our bunkroom reading. The rest of the crew was too excited to resist, and the partying began.

The remaining ingredient for the impending disaster was that the outgoing captain took the delay of his replacement personally. Even though he was a grown man, he threw what would have to be called a temper tantrum. Instead of acting like the ultimate authority aboard the ship, he sat in his captain's chair and fumed with anger. Even when he heard the unmistakable sounds of a party raging downstairs, he remained in his chair and didn't intervene. He was pissed, and he wasn't going to do a damn thing until the new captain stepped aboard.

Dennis and I couldn't see anything through the door of our bunkroom, but we could certainly hear the raucous sounds coming from the party. At one point, Pa came in and exuberantly told us that we should come over and join the festivities, but we wisely turned the offer down. After he left, the volume of noise coming from across the hallway escalated until it was suddenly pierced by shrieks and screams of alarm. These were followed by the rough sounds of a scuffle right outside our door. Suddenly Earl's voice boomed out in the midst of the apparent scrap, "Want to know what we do to boys like you in prison?"

There was a unified chorus of "NO!" from the crowd, followed by the sound of a punch being delivered to someone's face: *WHAP!*

"Want to know what we do to boys like you in prison?"

"No!"

WHAP!

"Want to know what we do to boys like you in prison?"

"No!"

WHAP!

By this time, we could hear the pounding of footsteps on the stairs from the wheelhouse, marking the captain's move to finally intervene, and his approach was met with shouts and curses from the crowd. The door of the deckhand's bunkroom flew open, a stunned deckhand by the name of Mike was thrown inside, and the door closed again. From the puffiness of his face, it was clear that he'd been the one getting punched in the hallway. He stood there unsteadily and drunkenly tried to explain what had just happened. It turned out that while Cheryl was making her moves on Tommy, a drunken Earl had professed his love for her and had started to push the kid out of the way. Mike, who was good friends with Tommy, decided that he couldn't just stand around and let his friend be disrespected like that. But when he got up in Earl's face about it, Earl exploded in violence.

Now, Mike wasn't a bad guy. He was dumb as a fencepost, but he wasn't a bad guy. He did have the largest lips I've ever seen on another person, but he was like a big lovable puppy dog. His dream about what he would do with all the money he was making up in Alaska consisted of a Trans Am for himself and a house for his mother. Again, not the smartest guy on the planet, but he had a good heart. So when he thought that his friend being disrespected, he'd stood up to Earl for him. Stupid thing to do—noble, maybe, but stupid!

In the hallway, the captain kept trying to talk the furious Earl down while Dennis and I advised Mike that his own best course of action would be to head right to his bunk and sleep the whole thing off. Sadly, he was too drunk to listen to reason, and he started to argue with us. Dennis had been a bartender in a Seattle hotel and knew how to talk to drunks, but there was no getting through to Mike. He ignored our advice and slurred, "I ain't afraid of Earl! I ain't afraid of nobody!"

Dennis responded, "Well, liquor makes a man brave."

Mike was too drunk to see the humor in that comment and rambled on. "I would've kicked Earl's ass if he hadn't gotten the jump on me and sucker punched me!"

We continued to try to reason with him, but this seemed to wind him up more. "Yeah, that's right! I could've kicked his butt, but he got the jump on me. I should go back out there and get the jump on *him*! I could kick his ass!"

The more Dennis and I urged Mike to give up this foolish idea, the more he convinced himself that he needed to do it. Pretty soon, it didn't matter if we were there or not.

"That's just what I'm gonna do! I'm gonna go out there and kick Earl's ass. He ain't that tough—I can take him! I can take him!"

He pivoted and opened the door to rejoin the fray. In an image I will never forget, there was Earl with his ham-hock-sized fist up in the air like the head of a coiled snake. Mike practically walked right into the punch. In a flash, Earl struck, Mike came flying back into the room, and the door banged shut to another round of shouts and shrieks from the gathered crowd outside.

Mike, his nose broken and his front teeth loosened by the punch, struggled to stand up. He staggered over to his bunk and crawled into it. He continued muttering curses and threats to cover up his sniffling and weeping, and Dennis and I shrugged at each other as we listened to the captain and others try to calm the enraged Earl, who was still bellowing threats and vile descriptions of what he would do to Mike if he came back out.

Eventually, everyone dispersed and the boat grew quiet. A short while after that, Mike's sniffling stopped and we turned off the lights and went to sleep.

The next day, the new captain relieved the outgoing captain, and the company that owned the *Spindrift* decided that, after the debacle of the night before, it was as good a time as any to take the boat straight down to Seattle. A good weather forecast ensured that we would take the shorter but less scenic straight course from Dutch to

Seattle rather than the beautiful Inside Passage. Although the crew was mildly disappointed to miss such an amazingly scenic cruise, we were eager to get home and away from this ship and crew that had become such a part of our lives.

During this steam home, the deckhands were employed to do wheel watches. We steered the ship through all kinds of weather, which was thrilling, while the rest of the crew prepared themselves mentally and physically for getting home. Lots of sleep happened, and people sat around and casually bantered about their hopes and dreams for all the money they had earned. In our minds, most of that money was spent in one way or another before we even set foot on the ground of Seattle. After such a long stretch of hard work, it was fun to sit around in groups in the galley or up on deck and just talk about nothing very important.

But not Mike. He remained in his bunk for the next three days straight. He lay with his face toward the wall, and he neither acknowledged us when we spoke nor answered our direct questions. Eventually, he came down into the galley to eat, and we could all see for ourselves how his nose now zigzagged and how swollen his naturally large lips were. He was still too tender to talk about the fight, so he went back to his bunk without waiting for a send-off from us.

When we finally went through the Ballard Locks of Seattle and docked the *Spindrift* at a huge wharf, the engines and generators were turned off. Instantly, the boat was as silent and chilled as a tomb. The cessation of those familiar noises was one of the most unnerving and uncomfortable moments I've ever had. We all gathered our belongings and headed out as silently as the now dead ship seemed to us. Any thoughts of a big homecoming party were eclipsed by the need for people to just get back to their homes and families, and Mike left without saying goodbye to anyone. A few of us made plans for getting together later in the week, but as we filed off the boat and into the awkwardness that awaited us on the shore, we took off knowing that we would probably never see each other again.

I've often wondered what became of Earl. With his lifestyle, I figure he's no longer alive. The last I heard of him before coming back east, he'd spent his money at a crack house and was threatening his only friend in the world, Dennis, in order to get at the last portion of his money—which he'd begged his buddy to hide from him. I assume that the drugs got him in the end, or maybe it was the Mexican gangs. Either way, his words live on in my head whenever I have a moment of road rage or get angry at strangers in public: "Want to know what we do to boys like you in prison?"

But I digress...

Hunting Squirrel
from Horseback

● ● ● ● ●

During our thru-hike on the Appalachian Trail, Ben and I began to notice in the registers at the shelters that there was a man nicknamed Albatross hiking just ahead of us. It's a tradition that, while on the trail, all hikers will be given or assigned, or will adopt a trail name. Sometimes these change over time, but most hikers pick one and stick with it the entire way. The first and last names of the outside world are temporarily shed and stored, and the trail names become your new persona. During our trip, we ran into hikers with memorable names like Teddy Bear, Halitosis Express, Two Socks, MRE, Dances with Bear, Bubbles, Pheonix (he kept it misspelled even after countless people told him it was *o-e!*), and Albatross, to name only a few.

For Ben and myself, the selection of our trail names came in very different ways. Since my nickname was already Bridge, I decided that I would stick with that. But during the first sections of hiking, I found out that my clumsiness verged on disability. I fell off bog-logs, tripped over roots and rocks, fell down for little reason, stepped into deep puddles, and even rolled down an embankment once. I got so frustrated after one particularly big fall that I asked aloud, "What kind of bridge keeps falling down!?" The only answer I could come up with was the London Bridge. And that became my trail name.

But poor Ben struggled more with his. He started off as the Druid, but quickly discovered that there had already been another Druid in the batch of northbound thru-hikers who had just finished. He couldn't have a name that had already been used, and he set off to find a more appropriate moniker for himself. That name found him atop

Barren Mountain in Western Maine while we were resting after a challenging climb. As we watched a flock of ravens effortlessly ride the mountain's updrafts, he looked at these hauntingly profound and symbolic birds and said, "The wind belongs to the ravens. And so I will call myself Raven's Wind."

But this set up a scene that was repeated almost every single time we talked with people on the trail. Each time we introduced ourselves with our trail names, we were expected to explain their origins. When I explained the reasoning behind mine, there was always a smattering of laughter and smiles. But when Ben explained the circumstances behind his, there was only silence and confused expressions. And to make matters worse, if we did exchange mailing addresses and use our real names, invariably the people would mess up both of Ben's names in their sendoff: "Well, goodbye London Bridge and Raven Wing. Goodbye Peter and Glenn!"

The trail registers and trail names are extremely important aspects of the AT experience because they allow hikers to communicate with one another, but the registers were nothing more than spiral notebooks in which passing hikers and campers left messages or journal entries about their experiences. Whenever we came to a shelter, even if we weren't spending a night there, we'd stop and read the entries in the register. Many times we looked for familiar names to read about their states of mind and levels of frustration. We'd met most of these people as our trips passed one another, but some were only known from reading the registers. For most traditional northbound thru-hikers in the summer, faster hikers left instructions or directions as to where to meet up later, and there were countless messages that showed that the hikers also used the registers as a way of determining how much faster or slower their friends were hiking.

When we came to the realization that Albatross was just in front of us, we started to hike a little harder to make up ground between us. We finally caught up to him and discovered that he was an older man from Virginia who had decided to do a flip-flop in his thru-hike. He had started at Springer Mountain, Georgia, with many of the other thru-hikers of that year, but by the time he'd reached Duncannon, Pennsylvania, he realized that, because of his slower pace, he was at risk of reaching the northern terminus at Mount Katahdin after it closed for the winter. So he'd made the decision to get off the trail in Duncannon, take a bus up to Millinocket, Maine, and start hiking south from Katahdin. This flip-flop maneuver ensured that he'd get credit for hiking the entire trail. So, instead of finishing up in Maine, Albatross was going to end his trip in Duncannon.

We started hiking along with him, and we found him to be someone who had a great sense of humor and lots of grit. We actually liked him so much, we decided that, once we finally reached Duncannon, we would stay a few days and help him celebrate the end of his hike.

Duncannon was a dingy and depressing Pennsylvania town on the banks of the Susquehanna River, and it had two claims to fame: the old Doyle Hotel and the Thelma Marks Shelter. The former was a turn-of-the-century hotel that had somehow survived as a flophouse and hiker hostel. It was famous because, for very little money, you could get a warm and dry bed, a shower, and access to the hotel bar. Many hikers looked forward to arriving at the Doyle and having a good time.

But the Thelma Marks Shelter was a more terrifying spot for thru-hikers. This shelter, just a few miles south of Duncannon proper, had been the site of a horrible event. Just a few years before our hike, two southbound thru-hikers—Molly LaRue and Geoffrey Hood—had stopped there for the night and were brutally murdered. The fact that there have been several murders on the Appalachian Trail is well known, but this heinous crime was so recent and so horrendous that most thru-hikers were terribly spooked by it. As a matter of fact, Ben and I had highlighted the exact location of this site well before we had taken the first steps of our trip. Like us, Molly and Geoffrey had been southbound thru-hikers, and when they stopped at the Thelma Marks Shelter after spending a night in Duncannon's legendary Doyle Hotel, they'd had the bad fortune to run into a drug- and alcohol-addicted drifter. For no apparent reason, he had brutally killed them, taken their gear, and assumed the identity of a thru-hiker until he was captured by other hikers who chased him down.

To add to the already terrifying mystique of the place, Albatross shared another story about the shelter before we parted ways. Like most thru-hikers, he had planned to avoid sleeping in the infamous shelter, but the conditions had conspired against him, and he was forced to stop there for a night. After he'd set himself up in his sleeping bag, he'd made the mistake of reading the registers. He said the endless pages of disturbing entries from other emotional thru-hikers were rattling enough to make him consider packing up and heading off into the darkness, but he stayed put, even though there was a pall over the entire place—it felt like it was cursed.

Just as he was about to turn off the lantern and try to go to sleep, an eerie fog began to spread through the forest surrounding the shelter. Then he heard the clip-clopping of hooves coming his way. Out of the mist, several horseback riders with rifles resting on their shoulders ambled up to the shelter. As the horses passed, the men—each one, Albatross swore, resembling a Civil War soldier—glared silently down at him. Finally, the last guy in line said in a thick Appalachian drawl, "We been huntin' squirrel from horseback for five generations, and we're gonna hunt squirrel from horseback for another five generations! You got a problem with that?"

Albatross answered that he didn't, and the procession continued on and disappeared back into the fog.

He said he could still hear them when he decided to pack up and get the hell out of there. As he tripped and fell all the way down the mountainside, rocks cut his shins and branches slashed his arms, but he nearly *ran* all the way to the Doyle—he was that spooked!

After Albatross drove off for his home in Virginia and Ben and I resumed our southbound thru-hike, we knew there was no way in hell we were going to stop for the night at the haunted shelter. We did want to stop there and pay our respects, though, so after the short hike from Duncannon, we stopped there and took it all in. Just as Albatross had described it, the entire landscape surrounding the shelter seemed bleak and lifeless. There was a darkness in the dirt and in the wooden walls of the shelter that was oppressive. We tried to read the messages in the registers, but they were too intense and unsettling, so we left in a hurry.

Each step for the rest of that day was easy, for we were fueled by the motivation to leave that horrible shelter far, far behind. We even

Last of the Mohicans

● ● ● ● ●

It was during late October of my junior year at Bowdoin College that my former freshman roommate, Logan, invited me to go with him and a couple of his fraternity brothers to a Dizzy Gillespie concert in Boston. I knew that the man was a pretty famous jazz performer, but the full impact of the invitation to this event wasn't fully appreciated at the time. Instead, I was more focused on the fact that, after the concert, I could hop on a bus and head down for a weekend visit with my girlfriend, Shelly, who lived in Newport, Rhode Island.

Because of the slower speed limits back then, the drive from Maine to Boston seemed to take half a day, and by the time we got to the club, I was tired of being in a car and felt all discombobulated from being driven through the unfamiliar city. I remember walking toward the small and unassuming music club and thinking that maybe I had misunderstood Logan about the event being a concert. But once inside and seated at our table, it was more than apparent that we were in an intimate jazz club for a concert by a living legend.

When Dizzy Gillespie began playing his trumpet, I instantly recognized his trademark swollen cheeks. As he hit the cleanest notes and produced magical sounds all night long, each break was a chance for the audience to give him yet another standing ovation. By the time the concert was over, I was not only exhausted from enjoying the jazz music, but Dizzy Gillespie was my new idol! So, when an announcement was made that it was Dizzy Gillespie's birthday and we should all stick around to celebrate it with him, I was more than determined to do so. A giant cake was brought out from the kitchen and we sang "Happy Birthday" to none other than the great Dizzy Gillespie.

Because the jazz club was a windowless space and I was enjoying myself, I had no idea what time it was, but after we'd eaten our cake and gotten in line for an autograph, Logan reported that it was after eleven p.m.! I didn't know the specific bus schedule, but I was fairly certain that the bus service to Newport ended around midnight. If I was going to get to the bus station in time, we needed to leave the club soon…but we were so close to the man, and I really wanted a chance to talk with him.

Shaking Dizzy Gillespie's hand, talking with him for a few minutes, and getting a personalized note and autograph was (and still is) an important moment in my life. I could not believe my luck. As I looked reverently down at his signature and his message to me, I had no idea that that slip of paper would disappear in the midst of an emotional breakup with Shelly in the future. But at that moment, I held it like it was the golden ticket in *Willy Wonka & the Chocolate Factory*.

It was now 11:45 p.m., and we ran to the car so that Logan could get me over to the Boston bus station before midnight. In those days, the dilapidated terminal was on the edge of the "Combat Zone" and not a very safe place. As soon as the car pulled up outside the terminal, I ran inside with a quick wave and went straight toward the Peter Pan/Bonanza bus desk to purchase my ticket to Newport. But I stopped in my tracks when I saw that the last bus to Newport had departed fifteen minutes earlier. In a panic, I glanced back outside to see if Logan and his friends were still there, but they were long gone—probably already on their way back to Maine! I had no other escape, so I glanced back at the schedule and saw that the last bus of the night was headed to Providence, Rhode Island, in about five minutes. I quickly bought a ticket and boarded the bus.

This was before cell phones, of course, so I had an hour-long ride in which to figure out how I was going to get myself to Newport from Providence. After all, I hadn't told Shelly that I was coming, and it was now after midnight. This all meant that I was probably going to have to wake her up and ask her to drive up to Providence and get me. I could not think of another way of getting down to Newport, so I made the plan to get off the bus, call her from the closest public phone, and wait for her in the terminal.

The bus rumbled down the dark and lifeless streets of Providence and came to a stop at the deserted bus terminal. I got off and ran toward the outdoor pay phones to make the dreaded call. But as I got ready to put the quarter in, the lights inside the terminal began turning off, one after the other, until the entire building was dark. Then a lone man carefully came out the front door, locked it, and walked away without so much as a word to me.

I looked around at the surrounding neighborhood for some kind of diner or bar to seek haven in, but there was nothing but darkened industrial buildings, an elevated roadway overhead, and vacant lots full of dark and sinister shadows. I quickly dialed, woke Shelly up, and pleaded with her to come quickly and pick me up. Groggy with sleep, she grunted that she'd be there in about thirty minutes—but it might be longer because she had no idea where the Providence bus station was. I semi-jokingly urged her to hurry.

After I hung up, I was completely alone outside the deserted bus station. I could see nowhere else to go and wait, and since there weren't any benches nearby, I stood awkwardly outside the door in the chilly air of that fall night. I shivered a little, but I didn't know if that was due to the chill or the dangerous feeling I got from my current situation.

The dry and raspy cough was far off at first, but it was long and loud. It reverberated off the concrete overpass and the brick façades of the buildings as it echoed down the dark and deserted streets. I couldn't see the source, but another round of coughing signaled that the individual was getting nearer and nearer to me. I looked around to find a place to hide, but there was none. When I turned to face the approaching invader again, a lone figure slid out of the shadows and into the bland illumination of a streetlamp. From that earliest glimpse, it was clear that the person was not walking in a straight line, but was pitching and weaving toward me like the proverbial drunken sailor. I withdrew into the shadows to avoid detection, but this inebriated and phlegmatic individual's uncertain vector was pointed right to me.

He spotted me and stopped. A vicious cough seemed to spur him on, and I felt my stomach clench as I realized that this meeting with a homeless man was now inevitable. The image of my lifeless, naked, and wallet-less body being discovered by my poor, semi-awake girlfriend played in my head, and I gave serious thought to running away screaming and shouting like some kind of panty-waister. Ultimately, however, the man came to a stop in front of me and just silently stared. When he had another violent bout of hacking and then spit up what looked and sounded like a mouthful of scrambled eggs, I decided that I should start the conversation. I went with the overly obvious and honest observation, "Jesus, guy, that's one helluva cough! You should really see a doctor."

The man said nothing and continued to stare at me. Then the whites of his eyes slowly grew larger and he said, "Aw, it ain't that bad these days. It's been worse."

His tone was nonthreatening, and I decided that, if I had correctly guided the conversation away from a possible shanking, I should continue that track. "No, I mean it. A doctor should take a look at that cough. It's too damn cold out here to be walking around with a cough like that. You really should take better care of yourself!"

The man seemed to enjoy the attention, and he smiled kindly at me as he asked what the hell I was doing outside the deserted bus station at this hour of the night. I knew that I needed to be careful about telling too much of the truth, so I just replied that my friend was picking me up—at any moment. The man smiled again and told me that his name was Chris. And then he announced that he would stay with me to keep me safe until my friend came.

This was the exact opposite of what I wanted him to do. A new diabolic vision of Chris somehow not only killing me but also getting Shelly out of her red Toyota truck to do evil things to her ran through my brain, and to distract myself, I nervously asked him to tell me about himself. To this day, I'm not sure how I did that without sounding like an uppity college kid asking a homeless guy how he ended up as a stinky and drunken street person, but somehow I did. And Chris began to tell his tale.

He was a Vietnam vet who had gotten married but had struggled with alcohol and lost it all—the wife and the daughter, the family, and his hope for the future. The way the man unraveled his yarn, I could actually feel the suction of how his life had gone down the drain. Like a skipping record, the tale of man versus addiction and the costs of that one-sided battle continue to be repeated each and every day.

Suddenly, Chris blurted out, "You and me, kid, we're the last of the Mohicans."

Before I could ask for some kind of explanation of this comment, my eyes caught the movement of something in the shadows of the overpass. Chris swung around to see what I was looking at, and we watched another solitary figure emerge from the shadows and head toward us. But there was clearly something much different about this person. Although I couldn't judge their body size or their gender, their movements were predatory and sinister. I definitely tensed up, but Chris immediately set off in the person's direction, barking ferociously. No, I mean it—he ran after this person barking, "Ruff! Ruff! Get the hell away! Ruff! Ruff!"

The other person took off running, and the two of them disappeared into the darkness of the night, leaving me completely alone again. I could hear Chris barking frantically for another moment or two, but then he went silent. The night suddenly weighed down on me and I wasn't sure what to do. Then I heard the raspy coughing start again, and, as much as I was still counting the seconds to Shelly's arrival, I have to say that I gave an audible sigh of relief that my protector was okay and was returning to his task of keeping me safe.

When he was back, I thanked him profusely. He shrugged, "That's what us Mohicans do—we protect each other!"

We continued talking, but I began to calculate inside my head how long ago I had called Shelly. I came to the conclusion that it had been far more than thirty minutes. Assuming a few minutes to let her get dressed and a few more to find out where the Providence bus station was located, I figured she had to be just moments away. So I stuck out my hand and tried to kindly send Chris on his way, saying, "Well, thanks, Chris, for keeping me safe. My friend should be here any minute."

He grabbed my hand and shook it. The man was absolutely filthy, and I made a mental note to wash my hands before hugging Shelly. But as soon as he had a hold of me, he pulled me closer and said, "Jesus, kid, your hands are freezing! If we were in the foxhole in 'Nam, I'd take care of you, Mohican. I'd wrap you up and warm you up! You're freezing!"

In the faint light of the streetlamp, I could see that Chris's hands were so stained with grime that they looked as though he'd just rummaged through a dumpster. So when he started to rub my hands between his, I felt a little vomit rise in the back of my throat. Forget just washing my hands before hugging Shelly; I was now going to have to take a shower!

As he continued to rub my hands, he bent over and blew on them, too. The alcohol vapors snapped my head back like a whiff of ammonia. The warmth of his breath on my cold hands was simultaneously soothing and disturbing. He kept at it and declared, "Your hands are too damn cold, Mohican! Don't worry, I'll take care of you!"

With that as my only warning, he yanked my hands right into his armpits. Even though I pulled back in revulsion, he had my hands pinned under his arms, and we were stuck in this dance-like pose when Shelly pulled up and honked her horn.

Her appearance prompted Chris to release my hands. Thankfully, I was free of him, but I kept my hands held high in front of me as if they had fresh nail polish on them. I was about to thank Chris again and sprint to the safety of the waiting pickup truck, but I stopped and did something that just seemed right. I reached into my pocket, took out the twenty-dollar bill that was in there, and I gave it to Chris. It was all the spending money I had, and I knew I would have to borrow all weekend and for my bus ticket home, but it felt like the right thing to do. Sure, the man was definitely going to spend the money on booze and keep the high going, but it seemed to be what Mohicans did for each another.

As soon as he realized what I had put into his hand, Chris reached out and tried to hug me, and I had to beat a hasty retreat toward the truck before he succeeded. He continued to croon about our being Mohicans until I quickly shook his hand again, opened the truck door, and got in.

As we drove away with Chris still waving goodbye, Shelly turned and asked, "Do I need to know why you had your hands in that homeless guy's armpits?"

I was still holding them out in front of me like a monster in a '50s movie as I shook my head. "Just drive fast and get me the hell out of here!"

But I digress...

The Shark

● ● ● ● ●

During the next summer, I worked at a lobster company in Newport, Rhode Island. The work in the ancient and decrepit lobster warehouse was wet and difficult, but I loved every minute of it. The camaraderie of working with society's forgotten people, each with their own collection of sad stories about addictions and missed opportunities, and the energy of one of the last vestiges of Newport's working waterfront, made the experience one of the grandest adventures of my young life.

But whenever an offshore lobster boat pulled up to the wharf to unload its tanks of crustaceans, I felt much less enthused about my situation. Actually, after we were done sorting the thousands of lobsters from these boats and they pulled away from our wharf to head back to the commercial fishing boat dock, I felt real twinges of melancholy and envy. It took me a while to understand why these feelings hit me after seeing those boats and crews. Then I realized that yes, I was having a bold adventure, but I was still trapped on shore. The crewmen of those offshore boats were *free* out there on the high seas, and I wanted that type of freedom.

So the following summer, I headed back to Newport the day after my college graduation to get a job on one of those boats. I went down to the commercial fishing boat wharf that protruded from the opulent downtown area like an ugly wart and asked around if anyone needed a new crewman. This wharf was a dusty area that reeked of rotting fish and diesel fuel, and I felt awkward as I walked around and talked to the captains and crewmen of the boats in port. Most of them recognized me from the previous summer of working at the lobster company, but they all had an established crew and didn't need any help.

When I got to the F/V *Thomas-Zachary*, Captain Johnny gave me a temporary job as the master baiter and bander for their next four lobstering trips. I was thrilled.

The F/V *Thomas-Zachary* was an impressive steel-hulled offshore lobster boat that was well maintained and successful, but what had made the boat and the captain memorable to me was the fact that Johnny was engaged to a beautiful young woman. During the previous summer, every time the *Thomas-Zachary* returned to port, Jo-Anne came down to the docks to greet her returning fiancé captain. In the grimy and gritty world of the docks, a beautiful woman was like a ray of sunshine. And the way the two of them embraced and kissed during their reunions was another burst of goodness and light to those of us who were struggling with the depressing aura of our own lives and workplace.

I quickly learned that the life of a master baiter on a lobster boat was not going to be a glamorous one. I was told to come back to the wharf early the next day to help winch aboard the dozen or so plastic fifty-gallon barrels of bait for the upcoming trip. The boat's lobster traps were baited with a mixture of skate, fish heads, and salted pogies, and we had to arrange the barrels against the port gunwale and cinch them down with ropes so they wouldn't roll around in heavy seas. To arrange the barrels as the captain wanted them, we had to see their contents, so we unscrewed the black plastic lids and looked inside each one to ascertain its contents. As soon as we did that, however, it appeared the barrels were full of puffed rice, not bait. When the puffed rice moved and undulated, we realized with horror that the tops of the barrels were churning masses of maggots! I not only gagged from the smell, but, as we screwed the lids back on, I was sobered by the thought that *I'd* be the one who'd be up to his armpits in that reeking, rotting, maggot-infested bait!

I had never been offshore on a commercial fishing boat before, but I found out almost immediately that life aboard one of these vessels wasn't really about freedom, but endless work. Our bunks were in the bow bunkroom, which meant that we were tossed around whenever the ocean got churned up. But that didn't really matter because we didn't sleep much during a typical four-day trip. The day's hauling through started at five in the morning and didn't end until ten at night. On top of this, each of us was expected to do an hour-and-a-half wheel watch every night, so we were sleeping maybe four hours a night if we were lucky. We ate huge and delicious meals, and we got some breaks whenever we were steaming to different groupings of gear, but the aching fatigue from nearly constant work was so thorough, it was worn like one of those lead vests that protects you from X-rays. The desire to get home and get away from the endless work contributed to our debilitating "main channel fever" at the end of each trip, as we longed for nothing more than to be ashore and away from the labors of the boat.

The other crewmen were all veteran fishermen and longtime members of the crew, and they treated me with the usual mix of nurturing and hazing. They made sure I was safe, but they expected me to pull my own weight. I did my best to earn their respect, and they did their best to make that hard to do. Their favorite game was throwing odd things at me that came up in the traps. I had to dodge starfish, snail shells, and sea urchins, but they loved it when there was something more lively. Once, they threw a wolf fish at me. I had never seen one before, and I was surprised to see a three-and-a-half-foot eel-like fish with a humanoid face and a nasty set of teeth writhing around my feet. Since these fish easily crush mollusks and urchins with their strong jaws, their mouths are a good place to avoid putting anything sensitive. As a matter of fact, the way this fish chomped on the metal legs of the baiting table and bit whatever got too close to its mouth was more than a little unnerving. After doing a little dance with it that greatly amused the other guys, I took care of it by slashing its throat with a fishing knife.

Another critter that they threw at me was some kind of deepwater segmented worm. It landed on the baiting table and moved like a giant earthworm. Just as I reached to fling it off, its mouth opened like that of an alien creature. I swear, it had a plus sign for a mouth and all four sections opened at the same time. I shrieked like a little girl, which of course drew hearty laughter from the other crewmen.

One of the trips had another type of memorable moment. The weather was beautiful, and we had a long steam between gear. During these pauses, we became incredibly adept at finding a little nook or a pile of something soft like coils of line to curl up on for a power nap. The air was warm with June sunshine, and we were all snoozing like cats when the captain yelled out, "What the hell is that?"

He was standing at the gunwale, looking off in the distance. We all jumped up and joined him. He pointed to something far off in the water that was moving so fast it had a wake of white water behind it. We shielded our eyes from the sun and stared as we tried to figure out what it was, but no one had an idea yet. Captain Johnny said, "When I first saw it, I thought it was the periscope of a nuclear sub or something. But then I could see that it weren't that."

We were on a collision course with the object as we continued to try to figure out what we were looking at. Suddenly someone yelled out, "It's a shark fin!"

As the paths of the boat and the fin converged, we saw that the dorsal fin was over two feet tall, which mystified the guys—what kind of shark would have such a large fin? The boat's speed slowed to match the fish's, and we turned slightly to travel in a parallel course with it. The conditions were absolutely perfect for seeing the whole creature— the sun was high in the sky behind it, illuminating the water with the quality of aquarium lighting—and as we caught a vivid glimpse of it, we gasped in alarm.

In front of us was a massive shark that was nearly twenty feet in length! The magnifying qualities of sea water aside, the body was nearly a quarter the length of the boat, and it had a pointed snout, a gray body, and a white belly. It was definitely not a whale shark, which has a square snout and a wide and harmless mouth, but we continued to buzz at the sheer size of it.

Captain Johnny said, "That's a great white, boys! I thought it might be a basking shark when we first saw that fin, but I've seen plenty of those, and that ain't the right color. It's not a mako and sure as shit not a tiger. The only thing it could be is a great white."

The shark swam nonchalantly along, completely unbothered by our proximity. The onyx-like black eye scanned all of us, and we joked that we were nothing but a five-course meal to it. Then, with the subtlest of movements, the shark slowly peeled away and disappeared into the depths like some kind of phantasm.

Later on, after we resumed our course toward the gear, we came alongside something white floating in the water, and we had to check out. Although it was nearly a formless blob, the stench coming off of it was terrible. As we caught a whiff of it, the captain told us it was the rotting carcass of a dead whale. We circled it once, and as we steamed away, the deck boss said loudly, "Well, I guess we know what that big shark was heading for now—dinner time!"

But there was uneasiness in the nods of the other men. When I noticed this and asked about it, one of the younger men said, "Jesus, I can't stop thinking about that damn giant shark! There's been more times than I can count when we've stopped out here on hot days and jumped overboard to have a quick swim. *Right here.* I mean, we were probably right above that killer we saw today!"

The faces of the other men blanched at this comment, and I recognized the power that comes when you learn something new about the most familiar of things. These hardy men made their livings harvesting the sea, but the sight of the great white shark had visibly upset them. They had been in terrifying storms, lost friends and peers to sinking boats, and seen creatures that seemed to have fallen from space, but they had never seen anything that had inspired the kind of fear that the giant shark had that day. And, I must admit, their newfound fear was contagious.

But I digress…

Huey the Lobsterman

● ● ● ● ●

During that summer working at the lobster company, I met a cast of characters unlike any I had ever lived with before. There were beautiful and rough women who partied hard and came to work with black eyes that they blamed on falling down and bumping into doors, drunks who made it through the day by hiding their stashes in walk-in coolers and cold-water lobster tanks, a midget with a predilection to stab people in drunken fights, and faceless and homeless men who worked on the wharf during the day and slept in the derelict boats on the waterfront at night. For my time with them, they accepted me as one of their own and shared their stories and their hopes and dreams with me, and I skated the thin ice of enjoying them without letting the addictive substances and the violence that were so prevalent in their lives to grab me and pull me under. It was okay to go to the fishermen's bar to hear my buddy play the drums, but when the drunken shouts of an impending fight started up, I knew it was time to go home. After all, I'd hear the gory details the next day at work.

Working at the lobster company was the first time that I understood the famous John Steinbeck quote from *Cannery Row:* "Cannery Row in Monterey in California is a poem, a stink, a grating noise, a quality of light, a tone, a habit, a nostalgia, a dream…" The ancient lobster warehouse was similar to that description, and the routines of the place soon set the pace of my own existence. One such daily event was when the local day lobstermen came in with their catches during the late afternoon. As opposed to the steel-hulled offshore boats that sidled up to the wharf looking invincible as their youthful crews unloaded the copious catches from their five-day hauls, the local lobstermen seemed to be mostly older men who pulled up in small, rugged lobster boats and dragged their meager catches onto the wharf in big plastic fish totes.

When I first met Huey, he was pulling one of these totes full of lobsters up the wooden walkway and into the lobster company. He had a full white beard that hung down to his stomach, and to me, he looked like a stooped old man who needed help. So I offered to take the metal fish hook from his hand and pull his catch the rest of the way. My coworkers chortled at this and made fun of me, but Huey just said with a twinkle in his eye, "Don't worry about it, kid. I got it."

Afterwards, I could not understand this moment of cruelty from the guys I worked with—it seemed mean to let an old man struggle with the totes like that, and I said so. They had another good laugh at my indignation and told me that I needed to wait until the hot days of summer arrived. When they did, they said that I'd understand the humor in my offering to help Huey. I refused to accept that explanation, and I continued to offer my assistance to Huey each and every afternoon that he came in with his catch, regardless of the man's rejections and the snickers from the other guys.

When the tropic heat of July did hit Newport, the shadows and damp interior of the lobster company provided the only refuge from the blistering sun. It was on one of these days that Huey came in at his usual hour, but there was something different about him that instantly explained why my coworkers had been laughing at me. Huey came up the walkway pulling his totes, but he was not wearing his usual long-sleeved shirt. Instead, he wore a shirt that had *no* sleeves. As I came over to him to offer my usual help with his catch, I saw that the man's bare arms had the muscles of a bodybuilder! His biceps were easily the size of my thighs and were chiseled with pencil-sized veins. I stopped and stared open-mouthed at a pair of arms that Arnold Schwarzenegger would have envied! I suddenly understood why everyone had been making fun of me—Huey was so strong he could have snapped me like a twig!

After his catch had been weighed and he'd headed back to his boat, I immediately asked the guys about Huey's arms. They informed me that the man hand-hauled all his traps from an aluminum skiff with a battered old outboard motor. As far as anyone knew, he never took a sternman with him, which meant that Huey lifted his hundred or so traps by hand every day. The man was as strong as an ox! And, as much as the realization made me feel like an ass for judging a book solely by its cover, I continued to semi-jokingly ask Huey from time to time for the rest of the summer if he needed any help, but he always refused with a gentle chuckle.

Years later, I was flipping through a Patagonia catalogue when I spied a photograph of Huey in his boat with a seagull perched on the bow. As soon as I saw that white beard and stooped back, I instantly recognized the man. The picture was beautiful and poignant, but I laughed because Huey was wearing a long-sleeved shirt, so his secret was safely covered. I wondered how many people looked at the photograph of the old man, and made the same mistake that I had, not seeing the strength that was just out of sight.

But I digress...

The First Tattoo

● ● ● ● ●

After I read *Heart of Darkness* in high school and learned that Joseph Conrad had spent time working on tramp steamers, I became obsessed with becoming a merchant marine sailor. Reading Richard Henry Dana Jr.'s *Two Years Before the Mast* and Herman Melville's *Billy Budd* sealed the deal for me. I was filled with youthful dreams of running off to join the navy or steaming away to far-off ports of call. And as part of that fantasy, I decided that I needed to get a tattoo.

In those days, tattooing had not yet received the acceptance that it has nowadays. In fact, there were only three echelons of people that got tattoos: members of the military, motorcycle gangs, and criminals. And even though my friend Anthony wasn't in any of these groups, he had a cross tattoo with a rose in the middle of it on his arm. So one day I sought him out specifically so he could tell me the details of where he'd gotten it and how much it cost. It turned out that he had been drunk as a skunk when he'd gone to the one local parlor to get a tattoo with his girlfriend's name in the middle of it. I had a ton of admiration for him, and the tattoo was the coolest thing I had ever seen. The fact that he soon broke up with this girl and had to have her name covered over did nothing to tarnish his image in my eyes.

As my desire to get a tattoo continued to grow, I even ruined a family dinner at a fancy restaurant one night by stating that I was thinking about getting one. Their reaction to this announcement was as I had expected. They said that tattoos ruin people lives; they're permanent, they hurt, they get ugly as you age, and they were the mark of lower-caliber people. We engaged in a lengthy and intense conversation, but my parents never actually came out and forbade me to get a tattoo. Instead, they said something along the line that they would be very, very disappointed with me, but they'd still love me.

To the ears of a sixteen-year-old-boy, that was a green light GO! So I started to make plans to get one. For a tattoo was not only the mark of a sailor, it was the chance I'd been looking for to finally get out of my parents' shadow. As the son of an Episcopal priest, I had lived with the whole community of the parish watching my every move. I never felt like my own individual, just part of a bigger goody-two-shoes team. And I thought that, by getting a tattoo, I would set myself free from all of this. After all, once I got one, I'd not only be marked as my own person, I'd have strayed away from the straight and narrow pathway of the preacher's kid that I had been forced to walk all my life.

So I went back to Anthony to get the specifics of tattooing. This time, he had much more graphic and disturbing details to give me. He said that he'd gone to Dick's Tattoos on Elmwood Avenue and had paid about thirty-five dollars for his cross. He described in vivid detail how the ink didn't want to stay in his skin, so the artist had to go over the area again and again until blood had dripped off his elbow and onto the floor. He even added that the whole tattooing process hurt a thousand times more than a bee sting! I didn't find out until later that my father had coached him to exaggerate and distort the details to dissuade me from getting a tattoo.

But I was not to be deterred. I had already made up my mind. On the next Saturday morning, I went to the local bank branch to withdraw from my savings account the twenty dollars I figured my tattoo would cost me. Because I had no way of getting down to the tattoo parlor, which was a mile or so away, I had to break the twenty-dollar bill by buying some gum in a corner store to get change for the bus fare. After the relatively short ride, I got off at the stop that was closest to Dick's building and walked nervously back toward the parlor. With each step, I had to fight my own self-doubt about the decision. Luckily, the entire neighborhood had received a recent facelift as part of an urban renewal project, and there was no one around to distract me. I regained my focus, and by the time I walked through the door trembling with nervousness, I was ready.

Inside the parlor, every spare inch of wall was covered in designs that were thumbtacked to the plaster on individual pieces of laminated paper. At the bottom of each paper were numbers that I assumed were a way to classify the different shapes and animals. Familiar designs of black panthers drawing blood with their claws, butterflies, dragons, anchors, crosses, and hearts lined the walls, and I searched them all to find ones that I identified with. I soon figured out that the numbers on the papers were the prices, and I realized that most of the designs I was looking at were beyond my twenty-dollar price range. There seemed to be enough other choices, though, so this didn't faze me at all.

As I scanned the artwork, the tattoo artist came out of a back room. He was your stereotypical biker type. He was a giant of a man with tattooed arms the size of oak branches and a belly that stretched his black leather vest and hung over his Harley-Davidson belt buckle. He had long greasy hair pulled into a ponytail, and he chain-smoked. His exterior was gruff, but his voice came out warm and kind when he asked what I wanted.

My reply was straightforward: "I want to get a tattoo."

He began to suggest a few things, and I kept making mistake after mistake. He pointed toward a butterfly as a possibility. To a boy of sixteen who was trying to differentiate himself by displaying a toughness he did not possess, the idea of coming back with a tattoo of a butterfly was beyond absurd, and I loudly scoffed at the idea. The man rolled up his sleeve, pointed to a butterfly tattoo on his elbow, and said happily, *"I've* got one!"

Strike one!

I continued to look for designs that were in my price range, but there weren't many that appealed to me. It was becoming clear that I had miscalculated. If I had brought another ten or twenty dollars with me, I'd have been able to afford almost anything on the wall. But with only twenty dollars to spend, the selection was much smaller. Finally, the man pointed at a rough interpretation of the 101st Airborne eagle's head. It was twenty-five dollars, but he said that if he left the yellow of the beak and the red of the tongue off, he could give it to me for twenty. So I concluded that a black-and-white eagle's head on my shoulder would be the perfect first tattoo. When he asked about the placement of it, I told him that I wanted it on my shoulder, but high enough up that it would be hidden when I wore a T-shirt. He took a Sharpie and made a mark at the sleeve of my T-shirt and set about getting things ready.

As he plugged in the electric coffee pot that served as his sterilizer for the tattoo gun, he asked if I wanted the word *Mom* put inside the design. Knowing how strongly my mother was going to react to the whole thing, I laughed out loud at this idea. The man calmly rolled his arm over to expose a heart tattoo with *MOM!* in the middle of it. "I've got one of those!"

Strike two!

He took a rigid piece of clear plastic with the design etched into it out of a filing cabinet and carefully poured powdered ink that looked like gunpowder into the ridges of it. He told me to take off my T-shirt, and then he shaved my shoulder with a pink disposable Daisy razor. He applied some Vaseline to the area, placed the plastic stencil on my skin, and pushed firmly on it. When he pulled it off, the purple outline of the eagle's head remained in place. He made me look at it in the mirror to make sure I was happy with it. As he said, once we got the needles and ink involved, there would be no changing it.

While I studied my reflection in the mirror, he took the gun out of the coffee pot and started it up. The characteristic whine of it made my spine seize with tension. Anthony had made the process sound like such an ordeal that I had brought some aspirin with me, and I now contemplated taking some to numb the pain, but didn't. When the artist asked if I was ready, I sat down in the chair next to him and presented my shoulder. I inhaled deeply and said, "My buddy says this is going to hurt like a thousand times worse than a bee sting."

The guy laughed. "Well, your buddy lied to you, man. It don't hurt that much. You ready?"

When the needle hit my skin, I flinched a little, but the pain was not excruciating at all. It felt more electrical or burning in nature, and once I began to get comfortable with the way the tattoo gun rattled my bones and the needle pricked my skin, I relaxed and started to get curious enough to start asking questions about everything involved in the process. I learned about the ink and the different needles; about how the outline was done with a single needle, but the shading was done with a bunch of needles bundled together. The outline needle was like a fine-tipped pen and the shading needles were more like a marker.

About halfway through the design, the artist's girlfriend came out and sat with us. She wasn't much older than me and asked me questions about my high school and the prom. I continued inquiring about the specifics of tattooing. I wanted to know how the guy had gotten involved with tattooing and how long he had been doing it. When I wondered aloud why I wasn't bleeding, he stopped for a moment and let my blood bead up on the outline. As he wiped this away with a paper towel, I was confused about why Anthony had had so much blood dripping off of him. I asked about this, and the tattoo artist explained how some people's skin is less receptive to the ink. When I told him that my friend had been drunk when he'd gotten his cross, I received a quick lesson about alcohol being a vasodilator and why drunken people bleed like stuck pigs when they get tattooed.

The guy began telling stories about the weirdest and wildest experiences he'd had as a tattoo artist, and I barely noticed when he switched over to the shading needle, which burned a little more. He mentioned how he'd recently had a customer come in and get a nice big tattoo. But after it was finished, the guy had tried to stiff him by saying he didn't have any money. So the artist had beaten the crap out of the guy with a baseball bat and thrown him out onto the sidewalk. It turned out that, when the artist snatched his wallet, the guy had had more than enough cash for the tattoo. This story was told so calmly that I think I gulped audibly. The artists and his girlfriend were being incredibly nice to me, but they were people that I definitely didn't want to piss off!

After about twenty minutes, my tattoo was finished. The artist told me to go and look at it in the mirror, which I did with great pride! The tattoo glistened with the freshness of new inking, and it looked beautiful sitting on my shoulder. The tattoo artist wiped it with Vaseline and put a bandage on top of it that he taped down with masking tape. He gave me very specific and detailed directions as to the care of the tattoo as it healed, and he warned me specifically about picking at the scab. He told me that, no matter how much it itched, I shouldn't scratch or disturb the tattoo, or the color might get ripped out.

I put my T-shirt back on. I was a bit overwhelmed by the experience, and my insides felt wiggly. I was very proud of myself for going through with it and enduring the pain, and I was grinning foolishly as we concluded our business. When the artist asked for his twenty bucks, I confidently reached for my wallet. As I did, I instantly remembered that I had broken the twenty-dollar bill to get gum and the bus fare, so I didn't *have* twenty bucks—I only had nineteen!

Strike three! You're out!

I croaked that I didn't have all of the money with me. I half expected the guy to grab his baseball bat and begin pummeling me, but he just let out a hearty laugh and said that he knew I was good for it. He took the nineteen dollars, shook my hand, and sent me on my way.

Outside the shop, I realized that I no longer had any money for the bus fare and I was going to have to walk all the way home. Not a problem. My shoulder was tender and my arm throbbed, but I felt totally empowered. When I saw a pack of potentially menacing teenagers cross the street toward me, I suddenly felt I had nothing to fear from them—I felt tougher than I ever had, and my newfound sense of confidence was unshakeable at that moment. I strutted home with the jaunty gait of a rooster.

It was quite a while before my parents knew about it. Even though I had to change my bandages frequently and take care of the new tattoo, I did so without alerting them that I had one. As a matter of fact, they didn't know for several weeks. My dad saw the edges of it peeking out from my shirtsleeve one night while we were watching television, but he waited for me to tell him, which I did on my own a little while later. While he was disappointed with me, he was quite fearful of my mother's reaction to it—as was I! As punishment for what I'd done, he left it up to me to tell her myself. Being a devious teenager, I waited to do this until just before I was about to leave for a three-week school field trip!

When I returned from that trip, my father reported that my mother had cried every night I was away, and that her fury was still very much aflame. She had threatened to sue the tattoo artist for the unlawful tattooing of a minor, but she had decided against that. Instead, she seemed to focus her anger solely on me, and my world was never the same again. She informed me that, if I was grown-up enough to get a tattoo, I was also old enough to do my own laundry and other life-skill chores. And I was forbidden to expose the tattoo in public. If my T-shirt sleeves were too short, I was to put on a long-sleeved layer. And if we went swimming anywhere as a family, I was to wear a T-shirt in the water. She held strongly to these edicts through the rest of my high school and college years, and until I was a father myself.

But getting the tattoo was one of the most important moments of my life. When it was fresh, it sat on my skin like something just drawn on it. But as time went by, the ink gradually settled in until it became one with the flesh of my shoulder. Eventually, it was so much a part of me that I didn't even look twice when I saw it reflected in the bathroom mirror. It irreparably changed my relationship with my mother and father, but it had accomplished what I had hoped for: it set me on the path to becoming my own individual. And all these years later, though the ink is faded and the eagle's head has been joined by other tattoos, it marks forever the day that I stepped out of the shadow of my family and took the first steps of life on my own.

I went back to the tattoo parlor about six months later to give the guy the dollar that I owed. He remembered me, and he called his girlfriend to come out of the back of the shop to say hi. He clapped me on the back and shook my hand and said nice things about a guy who pays off a debt. I left there feeling like a weight had been lifted from my shoulders, and I felt the release that comes when you do something that you dread to do.

But I digress…

"I Would Have Died for You, but Now I *Keel* You!"

• • • • •

After working on the offshore lobster boat, I was, no pun intended, hooked on commercial fishing. I loved the adventure, the danger, the discoveries that came out at sea, and I sought to find a way to get a new job on another boat. My stint on the *Thomas-Zachary* was only for a month, and after going on a fun summer camping trip with friends, I came back to the East Coast to look for work on a fishing boat.

The crew on the lobster boat had taught me the proper way to get a job. As I had done in Newport, I needed to go to the docks and ask around. They recommended that I go to Point Judith, Rhode Island, or to New Bedford or Gloucester, Massachusetts. These last three bastions of the dying fisheries of New England still had healthy fleets, and they were sure I could find a boat that would take me on. Ultimately, I decided to go to Gloucester, and I set out to find a job.

Fishermen get paid in a lot of different ways. While some get paid under the table in cash for the day's work or get paid by the hour, most fishermen share the boat's take. In this system, whatever money the boat makes is split by the captain and crew after expenses are taken out. The guys on the *Thomas-Zachary* recommended that, as I walked the docks looking for a job, I should offer my services at a discounted rate. If I said I was a quarter-, a half-, or a three-quarter-share guy, I'd be more likely to get a job. There'd be enough of an economic incentive for the captain to take a chance on hiring a completely unknown person, and then, once I proved myself to be a reliable crewmember, I could eventually become a full-share and permanent member of the crew.

But my job search didn't go too well. No one needed anyone, and most captains shook their heads and just walked away from me. But then I came across a young captain who seemed interested in my offer. His name was Captain Dave, and he was putting together a crew for a 30-plus-day longlining trip to the Grand Banks for swordfish aboard the *Catherine-Mary*. When I told him my experience included the offshore lobster boat and offered to go as a three-quarter-share guy, he seemed very excited to enlist me. The boat was going to leave at the end of the week, and I was expected to help load it with bait, food, and gear with the rest of the crew. I didn't care that it sounded like there was a lot to do or that I'd be at sea for a month or that I had signed on as a three-quarter-share guy; I finally had a job!

But later that week, as the boat left Gloucester's harbor and began its thousand-mile voyage to the fishing grounds, I started to realize that things were not exactly what they seemed. Captain Dave had assembled a crew of rather odd and perhaps unqualified men. Ricky was only middle-aged, but he seemed much older. He was a career gillnetting fisherman, and he had never been on a longlining trip before. Rocky was a big bear of guy with a good sense of humor and lots of enthusiasm, but he hadn't fished for swordfish in about ten years. His friend, Sean, a young guy about my age, had sailed on a few sailboats, but he'd never been on a fishing boat before. And there was an elderly man called Gregory the Greek who was the boat's engineer. He looked old enough to have worked on ships during WWII, and he spoke very little English. And then there was me!

We had to steam twenty-four hours a day for the next week to get to the fishing grounds, so we all began taking turns doing wheel watches and getting the boat ready to begin fishing. This included sharpening hooks and setting up the buoys and other fishing equipment. Because Sean was puking his guts out from a severe case of seasickness and was mostly confined to his bunk, most of the work fell to the rest of us. All the other guys knew each other from Gloucester, so I was the one and only true outsider. And for some unknown reason, Captain Dave took an instant dislike to me. He began to cast me as the scapegoat for anything that went wrong. Although I tried to work through it all, his nearly constant sniping started to sting. When he finally accused me of being the boat owner's nephew out to spy on the crew, I knew I had made a terrible mistake by coming on this boat.

After a week of this, I was glad when we finally reached the Grand Banks and could actually start fishing for swordfish. We ate a good dinner before we set out our mainline for the first time. The boat had a gigantic six-foot-long spool that stored well over forty miles of the monofilament fishing line we were to set out, baited with thousands of hooks, each night. At one terminus, we attached a metal high flyer that marked the starting point. Then, as Captain Dave steamed the boat in the direction he wanted the line to go, the rest of the crew worked as a team to put flotation buoys on it to hold it at a set depth, attached sonar buoys for easy locating, and clipped on monofilament leaders with baited hooks as it spooled over the transom. By the end of the setting, we had put out over thirty miles of longline that would free-float away from the boat during the night. Then, starting early each morning, we'd find our line and start hauling it in to harvest everything we had caught.

That first night was filled with extreme excitement. As we all took wheel watches and kept the boat pointed at the last sonar buoy's signals, we dreamed of catching a boatful of swordfish and making a ton of money. It was not unusual for each longline crewmember to make between four and seven thousand dollars per trip, so we were all filled with zip that first morning to start making some serious money.

We each had a task to do on the deck at the three or four different workstations, including storing the returning gear, retrieving the fish, and processing them for placement in the ship's hold. Captain Dave and Rocky took up position at the side control area where they could control the boat's movement and have the best access to the mainline as it was reeled back onto the boat. It was their job to slowly bring in the line, maneuver the boat, and announce when fish were on the returning leaders. In the very stern of the boat was a covered shed that housed the three leader/buoy carts. Two of these were mechanized carts for the fishing leaders. By pushing down on the handle that spun the spool hydraulically, the thousands of leaders could be wrapped quickly and efficiently. Also, the various buoys and poly balls from the line needed to be put away and the swordfish needed to be butchered.

On that first day, I found myself putting away the buoys and wrapping the buoy lines on a hand-cranked leader cart.

When the first call of a fish on the line rang out from the side station, we dropped whatever we were doing and ran over to grab an ice hook or a wooden gaff to bring the fish through the shark door in the gunwale of the boat and onto the deck for processing. We were all in position almost instantly because the adrenaline was flowing so freely. But we were all saddened to see that we hadn't caught a swordfish at all—it was a small blue shark. We brought it aboard and went back to our regular jobs, but some of the excitement that had been building was dampened by the bad news of our catch. Blue sharks have no value for a longliner, so it was a less than auspicious beginning to the trip, to say the least.

The same exact scenario played out over two hundred times that first day. To put that into perspective, let's just make the analogy that it would be like traveling to a remote mountain stream in the western United States to fish for rainbow trout and catch nothing but carp! And to add salt to the wound, because the pay-share system relies on catching sellable fish to make any money, and blue sharks were worth nothing, no one made a single cent during that whole first day.

So, as we silently brought out the bait from the freezer for the next day and went to the galley to eat dinner, our mood was already troubled. Captain Dave tried to explain what had happened as best he could—the Grand Banks was one of the richest fishing grounds anywhere due to the ideal combination of underwater shallows and the mixture of the cold Labrador current and the warm Gulf Stream, and fish of all types tended to congregate and feed there. Unfortunately for us, he reported, our longline had drifted into the colder currents, which had given us the blue sharks.

After we set out the mainline that night, the crew began to grumble a little about having had a complete waste of a day. While we griped and cleaned up the deck, Captain Dave spoke by radio with the owner of the boat, who was an infamous figure in the Gloucester fishing world. The captain was expected to call the owner every day to report about the catch numbers and the weather conditions. Even though we had only been at it for one day, the morale of the entire crew was dipping quickly, and we all knew that we needed just one good day of swordfish to wipe the slate clean.

Now that we were spending long hours fishing, the nightly wheel watches became more challenging. Sitting alone in the dark wheelhouse and staring at the monitor that showed the location of the desired sonar buoy was extremely boring. There were a few other longliners fishing around us, so the small specks of light off on the horizon were the only landmarks interesting enough to watch. The fact that we also needed to keep an eye on the radar to ensure that we didn't get run over by a tanker or freighter was exciting, but its novelty wore off after it was clear that the threat was minimal because we weren't really near any shipping lanes. Truthfully, the only break in the monotony happened just before the end of your watch. Before you were supposed to wake up the next person on the schedule, you were expected to go down into the hold to make sure the ice-making machine had not gotten clogged. This giant snow-cone maker turned the ocean water into ice for storage of the catch, but it made so much, it could bury itself in ice and burn out. Not only was this an essential piece of equipment for such a long trip, it was a very expensive machine. So, only after this extremely important duty was completed were we supposed to go and get the next guy on the rotation.

The second day of fishing started off sunny, but the poor fishing soon sapped all our good feelings. Instead of catching over two hundred blue sharks like we did on the first day, we only caught a hundred on the second. The only good news was that we did manage to haul in a handful of swordfish, too. While it was an improvement from the day before, we were all disappointed and somewhat mopey through dinner and as we set out the line that night. We knew that the boat owner was not going to be very happy with the news during his nightly radio conversation with Captain Dave, but we were hopeful that his anger would be restrained because we'd shown some improvement. However, when the captain came down from the wheelhouse with an ashen and serious face and told us to assemble as a crew on the deck for an important discussion, we all knew that some kind of bad news was coming.

He exhaled loudly and said, "Well, boys, that's it. The owner just told me to steam the boat to Newfoundland to turn it over to T.D."

During our steam out to the Grand Banks, the guys had told me all about T.D. He was the regular captain of the *Catherine-Mary,* but he'd been fired because he had a little problem with alcohol. According to the stories, he kept sneaking booze aboard and getting drunk during the trips. When the boat owner began searching the boat for his stashes just before it departed, T.D. started having a Boston Whaler loaded with bottles of beer and whiskey meet the boat outside the harbor to stock up for the month. The most infamous story about the man involved his getting so drunk on a trip that he soiled his pants up in the wheelhouse. When he realized what had happened, he merely jumped off the boat and into the water to clean up. Unfortunately, he hadn't taken the boat out of gear and it just kept going. Luckily, a crewman saw the whole thing, and they had turned the boat to retrieve their drunken captain. As punishment, the owner had suspended his captain for one trip.

So the news that we were being ordered to Newfoundland to pick up T.D. as our new captain hit us all like a brick. Captain Dave might not have been acting very nice to me, but I'd signed up with *him* as captain of the boat, not some drunk guy. As crazy as it seems after the way he'd treated me, I was loyal to him. The other crewmen shared this feeling, and we were all angry that the owner would pull the plug on us after only two days of bad fishing. When someone posed the idea that we could just disobey his directions, there was unanimous agreement that we could and should do that. And even though we'd be technically committing an act of mutiny against the owner, we decided that we would haul the gear the next day and steam northeast to the Flemish Cap to fish off the grid for a while with the radio turned off. If the owner couldn't contact us, there wasn't much he could do to us—we'd be over a thousand miles away from him and in international waters. Once we'd caught a boatful of fish, we figured he'd forgive all of our transgressions.

So, after we hauled our gear the next day and caught a few more swordfish, we started steaming away with the radio shut off. Two days later, we got to the Cap and found there were no other fishing boats out there—we had the pick of the best water. The first hauling through of the line proved that we had made the right choice: we caught more swordfish. Although the quantity was a little lower than we'd hoped for, the fish were very big. The math was quite simple: ten 200-pound "markers" were worth the same amount as forty 50-pounders. So we were quite happy to be catching some giants. After our rocky start, life suddenly looked very good of the *Catherine-Mary*.

Then a series of unfortunate events happened. First, Sean went down. He was still struggling at fishing while already weakened by his continued seasickness when he tripped over a stanchion in the deck and fell. He not only twisted his ankle, but bruised his ribs badly enough that he had to stay in his bunk to recover. Then Ricky hurt his back while he was pulling a massive fish over the side, and he was down for the count, confined to cooking for us, which meant that all the tasks up on the deck were now up to Rocky, Captain Dave, Gregory the Greek, and myself.

But the fishing was so good, we kept at it, and any concern we had about the mutiny was cast to the side as we focused our energy on filling up the hold with fish.

During this run, Gregory the Greek asked me if we could switch our wheel watches one night. It made no difference to me, so I agreed. After a boringly uneventful wheel watch, I went down and checked on the ice machine. The pile underneath the machine was pretty high, but nowhere close to threatening a clog. I climbed out of the hold, woke up Gregory for his watch, and went to bed. A couple of hours later, we were all awakened by Captain Dave screaming and yelling that the ice maker was nearly clogged. Gregory, Rocky, and I hustled down to the hold and began shoveling the tower of ice.

Captain Dave was furious with me. According to the schedule, I had been on the last wheel watch, so he held me responsible for threatening the $10,000 machine. He was so angry, he didn't hold back in his venomous comments, and he lambasted me even as we were all shoveling. When I couldn't explain the situation adequately without pointing the finger at Gregory, I held my tongue and threw my anger into the clearing of the ice. After the danger was over and the rest of the guys had gone up the ladder to go eat breakfast, I stayed down there to keep shoveling. A short while later, I heard the sounds of a commotion through the walls of the ship. The volume and ferocity were loud enough that I headed up the ladder to see what the hell was going on.

Everyone had gone into the galley, but Captain Dave had continued to rail against me. While the guys were trying to get him to calm down, it had slipped out that Gregory and I had switched wheel watches. And as soon as he realized what had really happened, Captain Dave turned his fury on Gregory, who sat stoically eating his bowl of cereal at the table. After enduring a long tirade of insults and abuse, the older man had shot up without warning, grabbed a large knife from the counter, and pointed it at the captain. With spittle spewing from his mouth, he'd yelled in a thick Greek accent, "I would have died for you! But now I *keel* you!"

When he rushed at Captain Dave, pandemonium had ensued. It took a while for the guys to finally get everything calm again, and by the time I got up to the galley from the hold, no blood had been spilled and all was back to normal. However, from that the moment on, Gregory was never the same. He spent all of his free time writing in his journal in his unique and unreadable Greek script, and remained noticeably quiet toward the rest of the crew, especially Captain Dave. He would chat with me whenever we were working in the shed, telling me about his job at the junkyard and how much he missed his family, but he was silent and reserved around everyone else. And, like some kind of oracle, he also began to quietly warn me of the terrible days that lay ahead of us.

●　●　●　●　●　●

But fishing stayed good and life took on a healthy routine. I was doing multiple jobs on the deck, but I spent most of my time butchering swordfish. This bloody job involved removing all the fins, cutting a hole around the anus, cutting off the head, and pulling the guts out. Each fish had a dark line of tissue along the spine that had to be scraped away before the carcass was washed and winched down into the hold to be covered with ice. In the course of the butchering, I became all too well acquainted with insides of a swordfish. The ping-pong-ball-sized tumors, the white segmented tapeworms, and the absolutely repulsive parasitic worms that burrowed through the fishes' bodies and into their stomachs—all of these turned me off from ever eating swordfish again.

But being the butcher also gave me access to the amazing and entertaining aspects of the swordfish. Normally, the head of the fish was quickly discarded over the side. But one time I got curious enough to do a quick experiment. Because they feed at night and at great depths, swordfish have the very large eyes of a nocturnal hunter. I wanted to see one up close, so, using my sharp butchering knife, I carefully gouged an eye out of its socket. Much to my delight, I discovered that once you scraped out the jelly-like interior, you were left with an eyeball the size and texture of a billiard ball. This made the perfect projectile to throw at other people—kind of like a packed snowball or an ice-ball. So I began to throw them at Captain Dave and Rocky, who tossed them right back at me. I gotta tell you, they not only hurt when they hit you, they left a good welt at the spot!

Most of the fish that we brought in were dead because of the specific way we baited our hooks. When the unsuspecting swordfish swallowed the mackerel or squid bait whole, the hooks ripped their stomachs open as soon they attempted to flee. But every so often, we did haul aboard a fish that was alive. As macabre as it sounds, these proved to be particularly fun for me. I'd gotten so proficient at butchering that I was able to cut open a live fish quickly enough to extract its still-beating heart. To feel the contractions of a beating swordfish heart in my hand was a humbling and empowering experience, but it was a lot more fun to sneak around and leave them near other crewmen to see their reactions. They usually screamed like little girls, which amused me no end. It does not take much digging in this story to realize that our sanity was stretched too thin on this trip.

Gregory the Greek was the next to fall. The two of us were in the shed one day, wrapping leaders on the carts, when he lost track of the length of one leader and had a hook plow a bloody furrow across his palm. Since hearing repeated horror stories about unfortunate long-liner fishermen who had fallen into the carts in rough weather, hit the control levers accidentally, and been ripped to shreds by the hooks, we always worked extremely cautiously back in the shed. But Gregory's injury had happened so quickly, there was no way to prevent it. And while the wound did not require any stitches, it proved to be the straw that broke the camel's back for the man. Ever since the fight in the galley, Gregory had been harder and harder to read. But now he became downright lugubrious. He continued to act friendly toward me, but his unshaven face and the dark rings around his eyes bespoke a man having a complete and utter emotional unraveling.

Meanwhile, after more than a week of good fishing, Captain Dave decided it was as good a time as any to make contact with the boat owner on the radio again. Understandably, the man was furious with the young captain and chewed him out mercilessly at first. But then he regained his composure enough to request that we bring the boat back to where the rest of the longlining fleet was fishing on the Grand Banks in time to get the benefits of the month's full moon. It was the main tenet of the swordfish industry that the fish feed the most on the nights just before, during, and just after the full moon, so the entire fleet was aligned to get to the fishing grounds around that time of the month. We steamed off the Flemish Cap and headed southwest knowing that we had redeemed ourselves and had succeeded in catching some fish. As we took up our place among the other boats in the fleet, we did so with renewed confidence.

But that was short-lived. In their very next radio conversation, the boat owner surprised Captain Dave by telling him that T.D. was on one of the other longliners in the fleet and demanding that he take the boat to meet that fishing boat in order to get T.D. aboard. We were to transfer him onto the *Catherine-Mary* and let him take over as captain. We held an assembly in the wheelhouse and, once again, voted to disregard the owner's order, turn off the radio, and head away from the fleet to catch fish.

As we began to assess the amount of fish already in our hold, we all did some quick mental calculations. Since it was a commonly held belief that a longliner needed to catch at least 20,000 pounds of swordfish before the crew made any money, and the estimate of our catch was way below that, we knew that we needed to catch a bunch more fish. But with the fleet sitting on the best water, we didn't have the access necessary to do that. In fact, we were going to have to get a little lucky to find enough fish. Setting our gear seemed like another act of futility, but when we hauled back the next day, we were surprised to find our deck full of fish. We had somehow stumbled into good waters, and we were relieved that we might just catch enough fish after all.

One day during this stretch, Rocky and Captain Dave called out that there was a big fish on the line that was alive and fighting. We gathered up the ice hooks and gaffs and assembled at the gunwale. The line was being pulled down with so much force that the spool was backed down to let out line—something we hadn't seen before. Finally, after an intense battle, the fish showed itself. But it was not a swordfish; it was an eight-foot mako shark! Unlike blue sharks, mako meat is sought-after and worth good money. So in this case, the fight to get the fish aboard made good economic sense.

During many a meal in the galley, Ricky had spun a yarn about the legendary ferocity of mako sharks from his gillnetting days. He'd seen three-foot baby sharks come aboard, get themselves upright on their pectoral fins, and chase the fishermen around their boats like rabid dogs. From the way he told these tales, it seemed he fully believed that a mako shark was a member of the devil's family. So now, as we watched this giant mako fight against the line, we were left to wonder, if those little guys in his stories could terrorize a boat, what would a full-grown mako do to us?

When the shark had exhausted itself and was up near the shark door, we sank our ice hooks and gaffs into its head and neck and prepared to pull it aboard. There was a pretty good swell to the seas that day, and our boat had swung broadside to the waves, so we were in a teeter-tottering kind of situation. In the trough of the wave, we were down closer to the shark, but up on the crest, we were farther away. I know it's not realistic to anthropomorphize animals, but this shark looked totally pissed at us, and its black and impersonal eyes not only broadcast a smoldering hatred, but also promised a violent and horrible retribution to follow.

As we waited for the right time to pull the beast up onto the deck, each man had the same thought pop into his head: where am I going to run and hide when we get this monster aboard and he goes ballistic? I could see us all scanning the deck for the perfect refuge, and I was determined to find mine before the command to pull the shark in was issued. When I saw the protected space near the hatch to the hold, I knew that was where I was headed. I also knew that, if anyone else got in my way, I'd have no compunction about tossing them into harm's way to get there. And that was another moment when I realized that the survival instinct can be one of the coldest and starkest emotions of humanity.

When the boat dipped into a deeper trough the next time, the direction was given to heave the shark up. We moved as team to pull it onto the deck, and then we scattered like mice. The shark thumped its tail powerfully on the deck once, and then—just like in Ricky's stories—it flipped over to be right-side up and resting on its pectoral fins. It unleashed its fury in a flurry of violent thrashes and a malevolent snapping of its toothy jaws. The strength and power of the fish was so awe-inspiring that I was frozen with fear in my hiding spot and grateful for its protection.

Suddenly, out of nowhere, Captain Dave came running out of the shadows with a giant bow saw in his hands and jumped on the back of the shark like it was a pony, and *ZIP-ZIP-ZIP,* he cut the shark's head clean off! To this day, I've never seen anything that rivals the insanity of that scene.

The shark's body made a few headless chicken-like movements and went still. We put the head into a bucket and watched in amazement as the eyes not only followed our movements, but the muscles at the base of the animal's jaw trembled and quaked whenever we came too close. There was a job to do, and we went back to hauling the gear in, but from time to time, I went back over to the bucket to see if those eyes would follow me and those muscles would struggle to get just one more bite, and they did. Finally, when I went over to check one last time, the head had become an inanimate statue, and I knew that the beast was finally dead.

● ● ● ● ● ●

We fished successfully for a few more days before Captain Dave radioed the boat owner again. The owner reamed the young captain out yet again and told him to rejoin the fleet to get another few days of consistent fishing in before it was time to start heading home. We followed his command this time, but we could tell that our boat was nowhere full enough to guarantee a good paycheck. And, although the injured crewmen were beginning to be able to do a little more on deck and we fished more like a team, we shared the sinking feeling that we weren't going to get enough fish before we brought the boat back to Gloucester.

When the decision was made to start the week-long steam back home, we were very conflicted. We'd been away from our loved ones for so long and had endured so much, yet we were aware that we would probably face legal fallout from our mutiny and a tiny paycheck. These thoughts turned everything somber for the voyage west, and our feeling of unease only grew as we got closer to land. So when we sailed past a small flotilla of local gillnetters just offshore from Gloucester, and they told us on the radio that our mutiny was famous around town and that the boat owner had hired some thugs to beat us up as soon as we stepped onto the dock, we prepared for the worst by making sure that we had weapons near us to fight back when we were attacked.

The harbor seemed utterly unconcerned with us as we steamed in and Captain Dave steered the boat toward the same wharf we had departed from over a month earlier. But as we maneuvered alongside it and began to tie up, a guy came running over and started yelling angrily that another boat was scheduled for that spot and we needed to move out of the way immediately. Between the tension over the threat of being beaten up and the fact that we had been confined to a relatively peaceful existence onboard the tiny self-contained boat for thirty-four days, the man's screaming and yelling so overwhelmed us, we just stood on the deck like deer in the headlights. And just when the moment seemed like it could not get any more absurd, T.D. came out of the shadows and jumped down onto the deck to talk to Captain Dave.

We found out later that T.D.'s month had been far worse than ours. The boat owner had flown him to St. John's, Newfoundland, to take over our boat. But when we'd turned off the radio the first time, he found himself trapped in that city. He was then directed to catch a ride aboard a fishing boat headed out to the Grand Banks to meet up with us and take over at sea. But we'd thwarted this plan when we turned off the radio for the second time. And after the fishing boat carrying T.D. couldn't find us, they started fishing for themselves. But they quickly found there were too many cooks in the kitchen with two captains aboard, and the decision was made to figure out a way to get T.D. back to the mainland. A deal was struck with yet another fishing boat that was headed to Newfoundland for repairs to take him with them. According to the tale we heard, the only way for T.D. to get from one boat to the other was by paddling in an inflated rubber raft. As he was attempting to do this, however, the captain on the waiting boat decided that it would be funny if he shot the rubber raft out from under him. So he opened fire with a rifle. T.D. was successful in paddling through the rough seas and the gunfire, but he was understandably not in a very good mood as he came aboard, and the ride back to land was more than a little tense.

At the time of his jumping onto the deck of our boat, we knew none of this. We were too stunned to react as the man just started talking softly to our young captain. He quickly explained that, since the boat owner was furious, the best thing for Captain Dave would be to disappear until things cooled down. When our captain saw that his wife had come down to greet the boat, he jumped onto the dock, got into her car, and drove away. All this time, the guy on the wharf continued to shout at the top of his lungs that we needed to move our boat immediately. I remember watching Captain Dave drive away and feeling helpless and confused. And the startled expressions of the other crewmembers reflected those same feelings. But just when all seemed lost, T.D. announced confidently that he would move the boat out of the way, and he walked into the wheelhouse.

We took up our docking positions again. I was on the stern with Gregory the Greek, Sean and Rocky were on the bow, and Ricky was amidship with the spring lines. The rear end of the *Catherine-Mary* kicked out, and the boat began to back away from the wharf. We'd only gotten out a little ways before the boat stopped for a moment. When we started going forward again, we seemed to be headed back toward the wharf. Gregory and I couldn't see much from where we were, but we could hear Rocky and Sean call out, "Okay, Captain, we're about a hundred feet from the dock."

No answer.

"About fifty feet, captain."

No answer.

The boat was moving faster and was going straight at the wharf we had just left. Gregory and I exchanged looks, knowing that something bad was going to happen. Then we heard the guys in the bow yell urgently, "Um, less than twenty feet, captain!"

When they got no answer again and turned to see if T.D. was aware just how close the boat was getting to the wharf, there was no one at the wheel! With a barrage of curses, they sprinted into the wheelhouse to thrust the throttle into reverse, but it was too late. The *Catherine-Mary* crashed into a smaller fiberglass fishing boat and instantly sank it. Our momentum carried us into another boat, and our bow crushed it until its gunwales met. By now, the wharf was a cacophony of yelling and cursing, and as Rocky and Sean tried to maneuver us safely into a space on the wharf, we backed so perilously close to another fishing boat that the crewmembers on it shouted at Gregory and me to watch out so that our fingers didn't get crushed when our boats collided. But, at the last moment possible, the *Catherine-Mary* was put ahead and the boat settled into the available space. When the engine was finally shut off, the vacuum of the resulting silence was filled immediately by the yelling and shouting on the wharf.

I was too much in a state of shock to register exactly what had just happened, but when T.D. came up from the engine room, he said that the accident wasn't his fault—that we had sabotaged the steering. Eventually, the boat owner showed up at the wharf, but he just looked around the scene and shook his head with the scowl of someone smelling sour milk. Even Captain Dave came back to the scene to face the fire, but by then, the craziness and shock was dissipating. In the end, the boat owner sent us all home and told us to come back in a few days to unload our catch. I grabbed all of my belongings and left without looking back.

● ● ● ● ● ●

But being home was not the happy experience I had dreamed of while at sea. I felt out of step with my friends and family, and I was confused by the fact that I really missed the familiar faces of the other crewmen. While I was gone, the world had continued on its course, and now it seemed hopeless to attempt to catch up to it. Although I wanted to be completely psyched about being home, I soon found myself tainted with a sadness and bitterness that made me want to leave again on another fishing trip.

On the day before we were expected to return to Gloucester to unload our catch, I got a call from Captain Dave telling me that the boat owner had hired a bunch of lumpers to unload the boat. If I wanted to get any credit for helping with the task, he urged me to get down to the dock. But by the time I got there, the job was already done and I had missed not only my chance to help, but the opportunity to say goodbye to the other guys. Only Gregory the Greek was still there when I got to town. A very young child with intensely blue eyes, who he introduced as his daughter, was hugging his legs while we talked, but there was nothing left to say. I shook his hand and drove away from Gloucester, and I've never seen any of those men since.

But the final insult came in the mail a little later. Inside a big envelope was an itemized expense and profit sheet for fishing trip #7 aboard the *Catherine-Mary* and a check for four hundred dollars. As it turned out, even though I'd been doing more than my fair share of the work and covering for all the injured crewmen during the thirty-four day trip, my three-quarter-share status remained unchanged, which meant that I got a smaller paycheck than anyone else. And because we'd only caught about 25,000 pounds of swordfish and some tuna on our trip, there wasn't much profit to share. In a cruel twist of fate, the lumpers that the boat owner had hired for one day made $250 each for their labors.

So despite the fact that I'd spent thirty-four days at sea with five other guys, weathered all kinds of inclement storms, fought demonic mako sharks, worked several jobs at one time, befriended a possibly mentally unstable Greek man, committed mutiny a couple of times, and destroyed a wharf in Gloucester harbor, I did not make much more than some guys who worked for one morning.

But I digress...

My Adventure with Bobby

● ● ● ● ●

During winter holidays when I was growing up, the family went down to Florida to get away from the long harsh winters of Buffalo. When I was a youngster, these were idyllic times of spending hours on the beach, swimming in the pool, and making new friends at the hotel. But as I got older, the appeal of being trapped for a week with my parents started to fade, and then it disappeared completely. Some of this had to do with the normal need for separation that happens within families, but most of it was because my mother was still furious with me for getting the tattoo. She would get so upset every time I took my shirt off and exposed that eagle's head on my left shoulder, I lost interest in swimming and beach time. Actually, to the teenage version of me, being cooped up for seven days with my completely uncool mom and dad seemed like one of Dante's levels of Inferno, and I was constantly on the lookout for distractions. Luckily for me, my friend Bobby and his family had moved to Miami Beach, and I was given a reprieve from my sentence.

Bobby remains one of the most interesting people I've ever met in my life. Intelligent to the point of brilliant, he is part of a family that has a genuinely comedic sense of humor. I have no doubt that, if they had all been born during an earlier era, Bobby, his two brothers, and their mother would have been a troupe of radio or stage entertainers. Because of their ability to laugh and amuse themselves and others, they've been able to survive difficulties and obstacles that would have lampooned most people. Just by living their zany style of life and sharing their weird and funny stories, they brightened every room they stepped into. That being said, the line between sanity and insanity in this family was sometimes razor-thin.

During one of the last times we got together in Florida, Bobby had the idea that we should head down to the beach at night with his telescope to do some stargazing. However, this idea soon morphed into an opportunity to look for naked supermodels in the windows of the towering buildings that crowded the beach. So, as we walked toward the beach with the telescope case in hand, the hormone-induced anticipation grew exponentially as images of nude woman coming out of the shower flashed across our minds like a peep show, and we jostled and giggled in teenage excitement.

The first indicator that the night was not going to be just an innocent moment of childish voyeurism was when Bobby told me to stop outside a convenience store and hold the telescope while he went in and bought beer. We both were underage at the time, so I was more than a little nervous as I stood alone and waited. When he came back out with a paper bag in his arms, my heart missed a beat as I came to the understanding that we had just ratcheted up the level of naughtiness with a dose of unlawfulness, too. I was no rookie at drinking alcohol, but this was my very first experience being around when a minor used a fake I.D. to buy it at a store. I was a normally rebellious teenager, but I wasn't exactly sure that we should be doing what we were doing. It was too late to stop now, so we continued more or less undaunted toward the beach.

We hadn't gone too far before a familiar car pulled up and stopped at the curb beside us, honking and flashing its lights. It was none other than Bobby's mom. She rolled down the window said, "I don't like you boys being out here at night. I don't think it's safe!"

We went over to the car and Bobby said, "We'll be fine, Ma. We're just going down to the beach."

"Well, I don't like it. It isn't safe out here. Here, take this gun."

She handed Bobby what looked like a snub-nose .38 special. He snatched it from her and looked around to see if anyone was around to see the exchange. As he tucked it into his belt, he rolled his eyes and said, "Geez, Ma, we're fine!"

"Well, I was a little worried. Now, you be safe, boys, and enjoy the stars."

We found a good spot on the beach and started to set up our telescope. The ocean was as black as ink, and the sand of the deserted beach was cold on our bare feet. Aside from the gentle lapping of waves on the shore, it was peaceful and quiet. Behind us, the high-rises were lighting up, and we were eager to start searching for our targets. We opened our beers with great fanfare, drinking the famous banquet beer of the Rockies, and the coldness and bitterness of them made us cough. Nonetheless, we toasted one another and drank heartily.

Two things kept us from achieving our pubescent goal that night: the demographics of southern Florida and the Inversion Property of Reflection. The impact of the latter hit as soon as we swung the telescope around to gaze directly into the buildings—thanks to the telescope's powerful lenses, every image was upside down! As we scanned the buildings for naked women, we had to contort our bodies to peer upside down through eyepiece. But even as we perfected this yoga-like posture, the real element of our defeat reared its aged head—this was Miami Beach, which meant that all of the buildings we tried to peep into were filled with senior citizens. So, even if someone was walking around their apartment with the curtains open, they were an octogenarian we sure didn't want to see naked! After viewing a few upside-down seniors in their boxers or shabby nightgowns, we lost interest and turned our attention to using the telescope to look at the constellations and to drinking all the beer. When it was gone, we trudged home disappointed.

Years later, the full reality of that night hit me: not only were Bobby and I underage drinkers toting a six-pack of beer around on our way to spy into people's windows, we were also in possession of an illegal firearm! If we had been busted by the cops, forget trying to count the strikes against us! I shudder to think what prison life would have been like. The fact that we were so amazingly lucky and didn't see a cop that whole evening is mind-blowing. But the utter lack of understanding on our parts about just how profoundly our lives could have been changed still staggers me. We went home that night focused only on the stinging disappointment of not having seen Elle Macpherson or Kim Alexis naked; we had not an iota of remorse about our stupid and crazy stunt. Ah, the foolishness of youth!

But I digress...

The Flicker

● ● ● ● ●

On a bright and sunny spring day, my high school friends and I chose to talk with the English and the biology teachers instead of playing the usual football games on the blacktop because these two men were two of our favorite teachers. While we were chatting with them about nothing in particular, a blur of color flew right at us, forcing us to duck for cover before it thumped against one of the big first-floor windows of the school building. The event was startling, but we dusted ourselves off and filed over the low fence into the narrow space between the shrubs and the building to find the culprit of the attack. On the ground, lying on its back, was a bird about the size of a blue jay, its wings outstretched in a crucifix-like pose. By the unnatural angle of its head, it was clear that the poor creature's neck had been broken in the collision with the window.

I had never seen a bird quite like this. Although not too impressive in size, the underwing and tail plumage were a rich mixture of golden yellow, and its pale buff-white body was mottled with leopard-like black spots. The bird's head had a gray cap, a beige face, a red bar at the nape of the neck, and a unique black collar and mustache.

The biology teacher said reverently, "Oh my, that's a yellow-shafted flicker! It's rare to see them up here in Buffalo. We're at the very northern edge of their usual habitat or migration routes, so we don't usually get a chance to spot them."

The English teacher inhaled loudly and, when he spoke, his southern drawl was like sun-warmed leather. "Ah, boys, that's the state bird of Alabama. Most people down there call them yellowhammers. As a matter of fact, the soldiers fighting for the Confederacy from that very state were called yellowhammers because of that bird. It's truly a rare honor to see one in these Yankee climes."

I remember looking down at the bird and being overwhelmed by emotion. Its natural beauty and the poetic endorsement from two of my most revered teachers was more than my pubescent wiring could take. Even though it lay there in the dirt and seemed to gasp and spurt for breath, to me, it was like a golden idol from a powerful Pagan deity, and I was swept up by the profoundly reverent hush that fell over us boys like a morning fog. After all, what was there left to say? The bird was as beautiful as anything I'd seen in my short life, the moment had been identified as a rare and unique one by two adults who had the keys to my growing intellect, and, at that very instant, words utterly and completely failed me.

In a move that was so fast it was a mere flash, Bobby lifted his foot and brought his heel right down on the head of the stricken bird and ground it out like a spent cigarette on the sidewalk.

The intimate and reverent moment of adoration toward the rare bird was instantly shattered by Bobby's action, and our outraged group of boys and teachers began screeching angry protests at him. He shrugged his shoulders in his jeans jacket with the lamb's-wool collar and said in a low voice, "It was suffering."

In the silence that followed, the sounds of children on the nearby playground and the springtime awakenings of the park across the street were deafening. I remember looking down at the bloody spot that had been the bird's head and feeling a deep sense of melancholy seep into my stomach. But acceptance began working its way into all of us, and we saw that Bobby was absolutely right. The only reason we hadn't done what he did was that we didn't want to break the trance that the beautiful and rare bird had put us under. The truth was less beautiful; with its neck obviously broken and no chance of survival, our inaction was actually a moment of cruelty. So, although his actions were startling, Bobby had done the right thing by taking it out of its misery.

The day that the flicker hit the window still haunts me. Whenever I see a photo of one, I shiver slightly at the memories of that day. Like some kind of Zen koan, the wounded flicker taught me some of the most important lessons of my life. I learned that sometimes the ugliest thing can be the most beautiful, and vice versa. I also learned that life is fragile—one moment you're flying gracefully and purposefully through the air, and the next, you're lying on the ground with your head smashed in. But most importantly, I learned that sometimes doing the thing that is most right can be a painful and unpopular decision, but, in the end, nothing in this world should have to suffer.

Epilogue

In much the same way my favorite radio show of all time concluded each of its shows—"Well, you've wasted another perfectly good hour listening to *Car Talk*"—I now find myself ready to apologize for taking up too much of your time. If you merely opened the front cover to skim the first few lines, you've wasted only a few moments of your life—consider yourself lucky! But if you read the entire book, I've taken away days and weeks of your life that you'll never get back, and I am sorry for that. I truly am.

However, I hope you got something positive from reading this little book. If nothing else, maybe it lulled you to sleep and you feel more rested now. If so, that's good news, and I'm happy that it served you well. Hopefully, however, it did more. Maybe it reminded you of your own stories. We all have stories. As I used to say to my students when I told these tales to them, they are all about mostly normal people in the most mundane of circumstances. Sure, something in them may have gone awry, but it was the humor, sadness, or enlightenment present in these normal experiences that makes each story memorable. What that means is that we are all sitting on our own treasure chest of stories from our everyday lives and childhoods. You don't need incredible tales of life or death, amazing accomplishments, or any other kind of overly sensational conditions to have a good story to tell; you only need to make some kind of connection with another human being. And it is through shared stories that we do this best—and we've been doing it since the human species first started using verbal communication!

So whether you tied your anxious dog to an outdoor newspaper rack and it got panicked enough to pull the rack down the street like a dogsled until all the papers had fluttered into the air and you had to buy every one of them from the grumpy vendor; or you broke off your only key in the gas door of your ancient Toyota truck at the gas station and had to go on an adventure around town to get a replacement made; or you met a homeless lady in a hiking shelter on the Appalachian Trail who insisted that she was part of the British royal family, a niece of Georgia O'Keeffe, and had run for the Senate with the nomination of a dirty magazine publisher (and had the newspaper clippings to prove each claim!)—these are the stories you should be gathering and sharing. As you tell them and spread their edges like pottery clay, you just might be surprised at how easy it is to connect with other people through your own stories.

As one of my favorite writers, Kurt Vonnegut, said in his book *A Man Without a Country:* "Electronic communities build nothing. You wind up with nothing. We are dancing animals. How beautiful it is to get up and go out and do something. We are here on Earth to fart around. Don't let anybody tell you any different."

Cheers to that!

Bridge